D0984272

A
Field Guide
to
God

A
Field Guide
to
God

A Seeker's Manual

PATTY KIRK

Guideposts
New York, New York

A Field Guide to God

ISBN-13: 978-0-8249-4792-7

Published by Guideposts
16 East 34th Street
New York, New York 10016
www.guideposts.com

Distributed by Ideals Publications, a division of Guideposts
2636 Elm Hill Pike, Suite 120
Nashville, Tennessee 37214

Guideposts and *Ideals* are registered trademarks of Guideposts.

ACKNOWLEDGMENTS

All Scripture quotations, unless otherwise noted, are taken from the *Holy Bible, Today's New International Version*. Copyright © 2001, 2005 by International Bible Society. Used by permission of International Bible Society*. All rights reserved worldwide.

Scripture quotations marked (KJV) are taken from *The King James Version of the Bible*.

Scripture quotations marked (NAB) are taken from the *New American Bible with Revised New Testament and Revised Psalms* © 1991, 1986, 1970 Confraternity of Christian Doctrine, Washington, DC, and are used by permission of the copyright owner. All rights reserved.

Scripture quotations marked (NRSV) are taken from the *New Revised Standard Version Bible*. Copyright © 1989 by the Division of Christian Education of the National Council of the Churches of Christ in the U.S.A. Used by permission. All rights reserved.

The names of individuals and the details of events have been altered in some cases to make them less recognizable.

Published in association with the literary agency of WordServe Literary Group, Ltd., 10152 S. Knoll Circle, Highlands Ranch, CO 80130.

Library of Congress Cataloging-in-Publication Data

Kirk, Patty.
  A field guide to God : a seeker's manual / Patty Kirk.
    p. cm.
  ISBN 978-0-8249-4792-7
  I. Spirituality. I. Title.
  BV4501.3.K565 2009
  248--dc22
                                        2009019684

Cover by The DesignWorks Group, Inc.
Interior design by Gretchen Schuler-Dandridge
Author photograph by Luke Davis/Main Street Studios, www.mainstreetstudios.net
Typeset by Nancy Tardi

Printed and bound in the United States of America
10 9 8 7 6 5 4 3 2 1

Many thanks to my husband; my mother-in-law, Anna Kirk; my friends Susan Vila and Ali Arant; and my writing colleagues at John Brown University (JBU Writing Women: Tracy Balzer, Gloria Gale, and Joy Kendall) for suffering through chapter readings as I worked on writing and revising this book. I'm also grateful to David Morris, my editor at Guideposts Books, and Greg Johnson, my agent at WordServe Literary Group, for their encouragement, insight, and expertise.

CONTENTS

From one ancestor he made all nations to inhabit

the whole earth, and he allotted the times of their

existence and the boundaries of the places where

they would live, so that they would search for God

and perhaps grope for him and find him—

though indeed he is not far from each one of us.

ACTS 17:26-27 NRSV

Losing Track of God

FOR TWENTY OF MY forty-nine years on this earth—spanning the time between my Catholic childhood and my later return to faith as an adult—God was not a part of my life at all. That, in any case, is how I saw it then. Although I had believed in God as a child, my sense of God's presence seemed to vanish sometime in my late teens or early twenties. Just like that. One day God was fully there, listening to my complaints, offering advice cloaked in fragments of scripture and song, imbuing my existence with meaning. The next moment the person I knew as God—the source of all knowledge, the counselor, the listener in the dark—was gone.

I wish I could name the day I lost my faith, the way some people can name the day they came to believe. Perhaps knowing the day—or, better yet, knowing precisely what event triggered God's absence from my life—would give me some clue as to what actually happened. Which of the colored sticks out of which my faith then was constructed so unsettled the rest in the pile that it sent them tumbling? If I knew, I decided in the nervous first years of my adult faith, then I could make sure it never happened again.

Was it my mother's brain tumor? Her resulting disability? My family's messy attempts to deal with it? Their despair? My own? Was it, perhaps, simply my age at the time, in my adolescence and early twenties, when many people question and some reject altogether what they had believed as children? Was I enticed away from God's side by things I learned in college or dismayed by some injustice I witnessed in my first forays beyond the cozy suburban existence I enjoyed in my youth? Was it my later experience of crime that clinched the matter? What circumstance, or combination of circumstances, could it have been that, on one specific day, culminated in my losing all contact with the God in whose nurture and love I was born and raised?

I cannot find this event, this day, in my memory. If it is there at all, I missed its signs at the time. Certainly I lost whatever opportunity may have remained in the hours and minutes and seconds of that day to find God again. On that unremembered day, I unwittingly lost the chance to feel around for a fragile foothold on the trust I once enjoyed—trust that the world was governed by a loving and real person to whom my existence mattered—so as to make my way past my difficulties to some more secure platform where I could rest and watch and plan another route.

Instead, trust simply disappeared, every rickety stick of it. Soon, God became a memory—or rather, an unexpected envy that came over me in the presence of believers and a formless longing that overtook me at certain times of the year or when I encountered certain words or situations that reminded me of what it had once felt like to know God was there.

In prayer, at church, in my occasional brush with scripture, all I sensed was an absence. It did not seem a temporary absence, as when someone leaves the room or turns away and refuses to listen. Nor was it the absence of remoteness, of a distance I had little hope of transcending. It was far worse.

I likened it to waking from an urgent but pleasant dream to an ordinary morning of duties and appointments and thereby undergoing a change of perception that I could never undo. It was the most ordinary of changes—waking up, as one does everyday—and I remembered the dream with only the most fleeting regret. How much of a morning does one spend wishing to return to a dream, however pleasant, however urgent? And so I entered the revelation of how things really are that separated me—forever, as it seemed—from an innocence I could never regain. One minute, as I tried to explain it to myself, I believed that this salt shaker was God. Then, suddenly, I realized that I was wrong. *How could a salt shaker be God?* I scoffed. And there it was. There was no returning to my previous foolish belief.

And there *I* was. Not the outraged atheist one sometimes encounters. Not a smart humanist fed up with besotted believers. Not even a plain old good person, like so many of my faithless friends, then as now. No. I had merely awakened. I was lucid. Rational. Bereft.

I continued to attend church for a while at first. Out of habit, I guess. Or maybe, even then, with a small, hopeful glance backward. But I didn't sense God's presence as I once had. I didn't sense God in any way.

Prayer left me last of all. Perhaps you would not call my prayers in those days praying but merely the babbling commentary of a child whose mother is in the next room. To whom was I speaking? To the toys and books that occupied me? To my mother, the source of these amusements? To God, the source of my mother? To the empty room? I didn't know, didn't care. As a child, I had prayed with the mindlessness, the self-absorption of childhood, never imagining that, while

I wasn't looking, the source of my happiness might become obscured or disappear. And so I continued to babble into the silence. Long after I stopped going to church or calling myself a believer, I still found myself speaking to God and then pulling up short—only then, in the moment of speaking, noticing the silence and wondering if it had been there all along. *Perhaps I had merely imagined the presence I had felt earlier*, I mused.

Here is an analogy for how it was. Imagine a world destroyed. Bombs or some other global disaster. An environmental collapse in which all creatures die, all life is ended. Picture a broken, abandoned, ended world—an ashy misery in which you are, as far as you can tell, the sole survivor. Everything is gone. Order, activity, all sources of power. Yet, unlike in most apocalyptic fictions, you are in no danger. There are no evil ones scheming to catch and eat you, and there's enough left of what once existed to keep you alive for a long time. But there's also no one to talk to. No one to take care of. No one with whom to share a scavenged meal. No one at all.

And so, you wander and pick through rubble and endure. You enter vacant houses, schools, places of business. You learn to find your way in a world where nothing works: where night is darkness and distances must be covered by foot, where water that you don't collect—from what falls from the sky or flows in sludgy streams—is unavailable to you. Gradually, you lose the habit of expecting these miracles. The miracle of the light switch, the automobile, the faucet.

Every once in a while, though, you don't know why, you pick up a telephone in some ravaged house and think, *Maybe, maybe it works, maybe my old number will ring. Maybe—why am I thinking this?—maybe the destruction I witnessed wasn't complete. Maybe someone will answer. Not the ones I knew then. I know they are gone. I saw them perish with my own eyes. But maybe someone else, some other voice, will fill the silence, maybe not even a voice but merely the sense of another living person on the other end, holding the receiver to one ear, listening. Even that would be enough.*

But when you pick up that receiver, there is empty silence. *The same deadness, the same absence I was expecting all along,* you tell your hope. The same empty deadness you have been living ever since the catastrophe.

Gradually, in any case, I grew accustomed to a life without God. Slowly, I stopped babbling into the absence. Eventually, I forgot to hope for or even to care about God's interested participation in my life—except, as I say, in those moments of envy and longing.

And so faith, when it came back to me, was an utter surprise—like the electrifying trill of a phone in one of those abandoned houses. The whole miraculous system of sound waves and wires not only working again, all of a sudden, but someone calling *me*. Knowing—or guessing or hoping—that I was there. Tracking me down. The abrupt and complete end to my aloneness.

God's company is a strange thing, residing, as it does, entirely in one's consciousness. One moment I felt myself alone in a hollow world. The next moment, without any discernible change in my outward experience of the world, I was alert to rich and abundant evidence of my Creator's passage through my life and ongoing attendance—evidence that had been there all along. I sensed God listening, eagerly, to my internal dialogues. Noticing and considering my every action and decision as attentively as I ponder my daughters'. Longing to intervene.

Faith, for me now, *is* that sense of God's presence and attention. Not just the end of the envy and loneliness and objectless longing of unbelief but a return, in crucial ways, to the faith I'd had as a child: the same confidence in the listening ear and concern of the invisible parent in the next room, the same dependence on someone else's greater power and knowledge and planning and efforts to provide for my existence and carry me through difficulties.

My faith now is different, though. It is less instinctive. I am more alert to evidence of the existence of God, more actively engaged in seeking and retaining a sense of God's presence. I cherish my faith more, I think. I remember the years of loss.

I have long regarded faith as a gift from God, something I was born with, as it seems to me, and then lost track of for a while but that God eventually located and returned to me. As such, faith is entirely outside my control. It cannot be attained through logic or arguments. It cannot be conferred upon me by anyone else but God, and I cannot create it. The bulk of me persists in seeing faith this way. I cannot conjure God. I can't argue God into—or out of— existence. No matter how hard I try, I cannot make a salt shaker into a being worthy of worship. If I could—if I, the creature, could create the Creator—then, as I see it, the concept of creation would have no meaning. I would *be* God. And I know that I am not.

Still, ever since my faith was returned to me in adulthood, I have been perplexed by those twenty years of unbelief. Did God take away the gift of faith, just as God surely gave it to me in the first place? Was God perhaps actually absent, as I sometimes thought? Did God, in point of fact, desert me? Does God, as Paul and other biblical writers suggest, abandon us to our sins, to our self-absorption?

A small but insistent part of me rejects the notion that faith is conferred by God and in no way fashioned by the believer. I hear Jesus chastising his disciples, again and again, "Oh, you of little faith!" Even the most faithful of Jesus' disciples—Peter, John the Baptist, Jesus' own mother—experienced doubt, after all. I watch Jesus confronting Thomas's incredulity—displaying his torn hands that had been nailed to the wood of the cross, parting his clothes to reveal the sword wound in his side. "Stop doubting and believe!" he commands (John 20:27), and I stand at attention. Evidently, I, too, have a hand in my faith. Some part of me knows that, in accepting the gift of renewed faith as an adult, I took upon myself the duty to nurture and maintain it in the face of the inevitable challenges that would follow.

It is that part of me that writes these words. The hopeful but wary part of me that won't wait, that seeks to solve things by taking action. The part of me that, in my years of atheism, yet envied and unconsciously yearned for God's presence but that wasn't even paying attention when my faith left me. The part of me that, to this day, loses sight of what cannot be seen and seeks constant confirmation that God really is there and will never leave me again.

I am like a toddler in a clothing store, exploring the exciting world beyond the spinner-rack of boring dresses but returning every few moments to my mother's leg, to the smell of her and the reassuring pressure of her hand on my head, to her familiar voice. It is this returning and reviewing of evidence—the leg, the hand, the smell, the voice—that protects one's faith, I think, and allows one to enter a world of distractions without losing track of God altogether.

Losing track of God is unavoidable in life, though. For some, God's perceived absence takes the form of spiritual dry spells, when God—or church or prayer—doesn't seem to matter much anymore. "Burnout" some call it, and they fully expect their faith to revive itself. It is not dead, to them, but merely sleeping. And eventually it returns. But it may take a while—sometimes a long while—before they sense God's presence as they once did.

My mother-in-law, a steadfast believer convinced throughout her eighty-six years that God is constantly present, recently told me that even she sometimes senses an absence.

"Sometimes I think I must have done something wrong," she said, "although I don't know what it was. Maybe I didn't give God enough attention."

For her, God's absence is the natural result of our own turning away—and quickly remedied by spending more time thanking God and thereby "letting him know that we need him," as she put it. "I just tell him that—even though he already knows it," she quipped. "And then, before I know it, there he is again, just like he was before."

For other believers, like me, losing track of God is more systemic and absolute. In such cases, God's apparent absence is not merely spiritual fatigue or temporary burnout, not a loss of desire for God or some other matter of the will. For me, it was more like what I imagine it would be like to be diagnosed with a terminal illness. Despite one's resistance to the diagnosis, despite one's surely enhanced desire for health and greater motivation to continue among the living, life recedes from one's grasp. In this way, for some, faith—or God—disappears altogether, seemingly irrevocably, and doubts fill the resulting silence.

The good news is that doubt is formative in many ways. Addressing doubt by researching the matters that occasion it—matters deeply relevant to who God is—invariably grows one's faith. Also, despite Jesus' commands to stop doubting and believe, he never renounces his followers for their inevitable faith failures. Consider his response when John the Baptist, in prison awaiting death on Jesus' behalf, sends messengers to ask, "Are you the one who was to come, or should we expect someone else?" (Luke 7:19). After Jesus sends the messengers back to John with a list of miracles he has performed—proof that he really *is* the Messiah—he tells his followers that "among those born of women there is no one greater than John; yet the one who is least in the kingdom of God is greater than he" (Luke 7:28). The strongest of us, in other words, may doubt, as John doubted. And asking questions and demanding evidence, far from being objectionable indications of unbelief, can be the measures of a vital faith.

In this book, I undertake to study the periods of God's absence from my life, both as a believer and as a nonbeliever, and to document the process of acquiring, reacquiring, and developing faith by collecting and reviewing the incontrovertible evidence of God's ongoing but invisible presence. All sorts of circumstances can cause a person to lose track of God and misplace the gift of faith. Locating God again—or, finding God for the very first time—entails actively seeking God's presence and then recognizing it when you find it.

Collecting evidence. Reviewing it. Actively seeking and recognizing God's presence. These are skills that can be taught and learned. Like all skills, though, they take practice to master. Toward this end, I have provided perceptual exercises at the end of each chapter, intended less as instruction than as creative opportunities. Use them as takeoff points in devising your own plan for discovering or rediscovering God's presence and attendance.

Whatever effort you expend toward perceiving God in your life will be worthwhile. Not only does mastery of perceptual skills in the pursuit of God's presence amount to spiritual growth, but, in the end, ardent seekers of God's company will find it. That's the pledge of the God I love. In the famous Sermon on the Mount, Jesus promises the crowds that "everyone who asks receives; those who seek find; and to those who knock, the door will be opened" (Matthew 7:8). God rewards seekers with the same confidence in an interested and all-powerful listener that I intuited as a child.

In the concluding book of the Bible, God's desire to be found is even more emphatic: "Here I am! I stand at the door and knock. If anyone hears my voice and opens the door, I will come in and eat with them, and they with me" (Revelation 3:20). Those who learn how to seek God—how to hear the knocking and the voice calling and to knock at the door themselves—will not only enjoy God's company but will subsequently know the way back to confidence in God's ongoing presence, should they ever lose track of it again.

CHAPTER ONE

The Frustrating Truth about God

For Most of Us, God Is Invisible, Inaudible, and Intangible Much or All of the Time

I MUST GET RIGHT TO the point about the pursuit of God's company. God is, first off, an all-powerful, all-knowing, all-present, and all-good force beyond our comprehension. Nevertheless, God is also a *person* and very approachable and, although not human, similar to us in many ways. Even in the Old Testament, which showcases God's *super*human qualities as "Creator of heaven and earth" (Genesis 14:18 and 22), God is routinely presented in intimate relationship with creation, especially with humans. God does not merely wield power over creation but interacts with it. God is capable of—indeed, is the very essence of—parental love: "As a mother comforts her child,/so will I comfort you," God says in Isaiah 66:13.

As the divine parent of humankind, God is as attentive to our needs and even desires as we are to the needs and desires of our own children. And, just as those human children created in God's image experience a wide range of emotions, God also experiences emotion. Indeed, in Exodus, God comes down to Moses in a cloud and passes in front of him, proclaiming,

> "The LORD, the LORD, the compassionate and gra-
> cious God, slow to anger, abounding in love and
> faithfulness, maintaining love to thousands, and for-
> giving wickedness, rebellion and sin. Yet he does not
> leave the guilty unpunished; he punishes the children
> and their children for the sin of the parents to the
> third and fourth generation." (Exodus 34:6–7)

Just about every word of this divine self-definition reveals human-
sounding emotions and responses on God's part. Some of the emotions God chooses to focus on here, you'll notice, are ones we
generally disapprove of. God is not only compassionate, gracious, loving, and forgiving, but angry—albeit with reluctance and not without good cause—and uncompromising, when it comes to punishing
wrong. And jealous, as God emphasizes a bit later in the same conversation with Moses: "the LORD, whose name is Jealous, is a jealous
God" (Exodus 34:14). Most astonishing to me, God, like any human
parent, suffers pain and regret: "The LORD regretted that he had
made human beings on the earth, and his heart was deeply troubled"
(Genesis 6:6).

The God of scripture, in other words, is not only supremely just
and powerful but a person we can get close to and understand because,
having been made in God's image, we humans are like God in essential
ways. We, too, suffer on behalf of our children. We get angry at them
and punish them and long to forgive them. We're jealous of their love
and attention. Sometimes, we're compassionate and gracious. Like God,
we love and want to be loved back. The God of the Bible is a God we
can relate to: not merely a creative force or "supreme being," as some
say, but a person with whom we can be in relationship. Like the best of
parents, God pays attention to humans individually, communicating

not only with a selection of favorites—not just with Abraham and Hagar, Mary and Paul—but with each of us.

But. This is such a big *but* that I want to ponder it before I go on.

I have always told my children—and, more important, myself—that the conjunction *but* should never be used in combination with verbs like *love* and *forgive*. "I forgive you, but . . ." means I *haven't* forgiven you. "I love you, but . . ." undoes any love the speaker may have meant to communicate. My personal commandment not to undo positive emotional messages with negative ones is so important to me that, in writing workshops when I teach my students how to respond to one another's writing, I tell them to offer first a concrete, positive response and *then* critique what didn't work.

"Critique in a new paragraph entirely unconnected to the first, preferably with white space between the two. This is a life skill," I rant by way of justification for what they see as a nitpicky requirement about an unimportant chore of the course. "You'll need it in marriage, in parenting, in friendships."

After the lesson, I collect their next responses to one another's writing and grade them on how successfully they followed my instructions. I grade their responses again later in the semester, usually more than once. It always surprises me, despite my own struggles in this area, how difficult my students find it to practice unconditional approval. Not a few of them—and among these often the most kindhearted—get consistently bad grades on their responses. Some transition word slips into their approval that links it to the critique that follows: a "but" disguised as a "however" or a "nevertheless" or a "that said." It is so hard to dissociate the good from the bad that many of my students, thinking to thwart my militant instruction, leave off the critical section altogether, for which they also lose points.

This exercise benefits not only them but me, reminding me to practice what I preach. In teaching—as in parenting, wifing, daughter-in-lawing, friending, and every sort of loving I undertake—I tend to fall into the same bad habits of conditional approval or, worse, no approval at all but merely sour criticism of everything my loved ones do wrong.

So, getting back to that *but* connecting God's more loveable qualities with those that I find frustrating, God is a person who loves and forgives and gets as angry as a parent and as jealous as a lover, a person very much like us with whom we can be in intimate relationship, a person who interacts with us daily, minute to minute even. *But*, most of us cannot use our God-given senses to know that God is even there. We can't see, hear, smell, or feel God. We can't hug God, hold hands with God, give God a piggyback ride around the yard. We can't carry actual pictures of God in our wallets. When God talks, there are no sound waves involved, no discernible movement of lips and tongue—not even facial expressions or gesturing, as there would be in a conversation between two people who are deaf.

In church services I have attended, we sometimes sing a popular contemporary worship song by Joey Holder,[1] the lyrics of which are taken almost verbatim—the only changes Holder makes are repetitions of key phrases—from an atypically celebratory and songlike sentence in Paul's first letter to Timothy: "Now unto the King eternal, immortal, invisible, the only wise God, be honour and glory for ever and ever. Amen" (I:17 KJV). Although I like this song a lot—the jolly tune, the meaningful repetition, the fact that the lyrics come directly from scripture—I nevertheless balk at praising God by merrily singing, "Unto the King invisible!" Invisibility is surely one of God's least likable characteristics, a key aspect of what *separates* me from God rather than what draws the two of us closer together. Singing a cheery song about God's physical unavailability is like singing one about a parent's perpetual absence from home. I guess I haven't yet gotten to that place in my faith where I can regard God's immateriality as laudable. Or appreciate it as a song-worthy trait.

Consider. As a lifelong cook, I love to share the food I have cooked with those I love and even with those I don't love. There is no joy like placing a dish of food before people that connects me to them. Nothing so reconciles. Nothing so unites. Cooking for people is a key way in which I express love. But, *but,* I can't cook for God. I can't watch God taste and chew and enjoy a dish that I have made. That is, in fact, my primary fantasy of heaven: to one day get to cook a meal for God. To make something simple and wonderful—good chewy, crusty bread and a goopy dish of eggplant roasted with blue cheese and tomatoes, perhaps. To refill God's wine glass and clink glasses at the table. To not merely *say* grace but to *share* the amazing grace of eating together. In this world, it grieves me to say, this ultimate experience of companionship with God is unattainable.

Or, attainable only by proxy. When I entertain a fellow human being who is hungry or thirsty or a stranger, Jesus explains, I am vicariously feeding Jesus himself: "Truly I tell you, whatever you did for one of the least of these brothers and sisters of mine, you did for me" (Matthew 25:40). Which is nice, but, forgive my audacity, not quite a realization of my fantasy of feeding God.

It is possible to believe in God without sensing God's presence a good deal of the time, but it takes more effort—as we will see when we take up, in a later chapter, Mother Teresa's heartbreaking confessions of God's apparent absence from her life. It is also possible *not* to believe in God despite witnessing evidence of God's interactive presence. This is demonstrated in scripture again and again. After personally experiencing God's terrifying presence, the Egyptian Pharaoh begs Moses to leave town. After observing proof that God exists, sailors throw Jonah overboard. Although the Pharaoh and the sailors don't appear to share Moses' and Jonah's faith, they nevertheless noted God's influence, not only in Moses' and Jonah's lives but their own. A recognition of God's active and current presence in one's life, in other words, is not a prerequisite to believing in God's existence. However, noticing God sure makes faith easier, if one does believe, and, for those who *don't* already believe, a consciousness of God's presence can be a catalyst to coming to faith.

Even so, a crucial—and, to me, sad—reality of faith in God is that the object of our worship and love, the power in which we place our trust, is invisible, inaudible, and intangible. I don't want to emphasize this *too* much. That God is, as most Christians believe, all spirit—entirely without a visible or tangible body or a hearable voice—is not creedal for me. I frankly don't know what to make of Jesus' claim that "No one has seen the Father except the one who is from God; only he has seen the Father" (John 6:46). I'm mightily swayed to think otherwise by all those passages in the Old Testament where the patriarchs as well as the lesser faithful like Cain and Sarah engage in actual conversations and have what sound like bodily encounters with God.

When God invites Moses, Aaron, Moses' sons Nadab and Abihu (the same sons whom God will later consume in a fire for incorrectly performing a sacrifice in Leviticus 10) and seventy elders up to Mount Sinai, we're told that they "saw the God of Israel. Under his feet was something like a pavement made of lapis lazuli, as bright blue as the sky. But God did not raise his hand against these leaders of the Israelites; they saw God, and they ate and drank" (Exodus 24:10–11). They *saw* God, according to the writer of Exodus. What they actually saw may not have looked the way they—or we—might have expected God to look, and the Israelites waiting below saw something else entirely, something that "looked like a consuming fire on top of the mountain" (24:17). But at least they all saw *something*, and they knew it was God.

Even today, many claim similarly corporeal encounters with God, and who am I to argue that they are not real? Although Jesus' discernible, bodily participation in our world ended after his ascension, I have known at least two reliable-seeming people who claim to have actually seen Jesus in the flesh, and once I heard a very convincing and solidly Baptist pastor say that God had spoken to him through visible messages in the air, as in those medieval paintings of Mary's visitation by the angel Gabriel. I want to honor such experiences of fellow believers—or at least suspend my disbelief—and not discredit them, as some people and sometimes even I myself routinely dismiss the little miracles of a day as misperceptions.

It's important to remember that we believe in the existence of many people we can't see or touch or hear speak. Often we believe in them because we did see them once or because we've seen their images captured on film or canvas or via some other medium of depiction. But we also believe in many people for whom we have no tangible proofs of existence besides stories. Sacagawea, for example, or Attila the Hun. Many of us believe in the actual existence of Adam and Eve, even though doing so contradicts much of what we believe scientifically to have happened in the beginning of human existence. I believe in some people's existence from statistical data, such as how many live in China, what languages have dwindled to just a few speakers, or the prevalence of Alzheimer's disease among the elderly.

Suffice it for me to admit that part of my believing self hopes, however unreasonably, that someday the imperceptibility of God will prove wrong. Someday, in this life, God—all spirit or not—will appear before me, and I will bodily experience God's presence. I fantasize that God will walk with me in my garden or reason with me

—that I will hear God's actual voice, as Cain and Sarah and Moses seem to have. It would be okay with me if I heard from God through an angel, as Mary and the shepherds and others did. Or, like Joseph, in a clearly prophetic dream. Or even, as that one pastor experiences God, through strings of words spiraling through the air. At least such experiences of God's presence are concrete. For now, God's interaction with me amounts to the moments in a day when scripture and experience coincide in my mind as one voice, God's voice, inviting confidences and offering counsel.

God's physical inaccessibility to me—given that my primary faith resource has God strolling through creation in the cool of the day and reasoning with Cain and comforting Hagar in the desert—is, in short, mysterious, as are so many realities of what I believe. Such as why, if we are *incapable* of doing good, we are commanded to *do* good. And how is it that Jesus, who *is* God, "increased in wisdom" (Luke 2:52) or felt "forsaken" by God (Matthew 27:46)? I may never be able to answer these questions to my own satisfaction, much less to anyone else's. All I can say is that a fundamental difficulty seems to be built into faith: We are required not only to believe in but to love God without the sensory tools with which we experience and love other humans. Without seeing God's face or hearing God's voice. Without smelling God's comforting fragrance or touching our lips to God's in ecstasy. Without wiping away each other's tears.

That doesn't mean we can't sense God's attendance in our lives, though. As a rule, bodily presence is not the only evidence that someone is there. When I come home from the university where I work, even if the house seems empty when I arrive, I can nevertheless tell right away whether either of my teenage daughters is home and often what kind of mood she is in. Hidden in their rooms with their doors shut, they are invisible and inaudible. Yet, I sense their presence in the roar of the heat/air conditioning unit and the jackets and book bags tossed on furniture in the living room, which is supposed to be my study. I find the remains of their after-school snacks on the kitchen table—or, if they are unfriendly with each other that day, in two different rooms. I can gauge their moods from how long it takes them to make their invisible presence known through muted music or by suddenly materializing beside me to ask what's for dinner.

Even when my daughters are not home at all, I am still aware of their continuing presence in my life in countless ways. When I make the rounds of their rooms to locate the house phones and collect whatever dishes may have found their way there and pick up dirty clothes, my absent daughters are all too present. I smell the hairspray Charlotte used that morning and hear the whirring of hot-natured Lulu's ceiling fan, even if it's freezing out. I see the splayed books and magazines they're currently reading and sometimes intercept an instant-messaged conversation with friends on a computer that one or the other forgot to turn off. Out at the road, the mailbox is full of college recruitment letters and pleas from animal charities and phone bills—more tangible evidence of my daughters' invisible presence.

Without meaning to, I fix Charlotte and Lulu in my consciousness on an ongoing basis. I record their schedules to keep track of where they are. I ponder things they've said to me, recently and in the past. I post their essays on the refrigerator. I sort through the clothes they outgrow, saving a few especially representative items for posterity. Even in the night, when I should be asleep and blessedly unconscious of their own sleeping bodies a few yards away from mine, I wake and worry about current or potential crises of which their existence is invariably the source.

If one of my daughters mysteriously disappeared or ran away from home or died, God forbid, someone who expected her to be somewhere at a certain time would likely contact me. I might hear from someone who had witnessed whatever event caused the disappearance. Even if I didn't, if one of my girls disappeared without a trace, I would know the reality of her one-time presence—as indisputable as any that could be seen or heard or touched—in the very pain of her absence.

In summary, I don't need my daughters to be bodily in attendance to credit their presence in my life. All I have to do is notice the evidence they deposit everywhere they go.

The same is true of God. God's "room" is the whole of creation —which, as Paul tells us, serves as incontestable evidence of God's existence: "For since the creation of the world God's invisible qualities—his eternal power and divine nature—have been clearly seen, being understood from what has been made, so that people are without excuse" (Romans 1:20). Countless indications of God's ongoing presence—God's daily activities, memorable acts, and long-term plans—are archived in the Bible. And my own life, even the portion of it when I was far from God—is a testimony to God's existence, if I can learn to see it so, as are the life stories and testimonies of other believers. To be aware of God's invisible presence in our lives—every aspect of it, all the time—we just need to learn to pay attention to the evidence.

1 ✌ List as many pieces of evidence as you can that testify to the existence of someone you care about who is not currently present. Even if the person is not someone you live with, even if the person is no longer living, go through your house and any other space that might evoke the person and look for objects and circumstances that testify to that person's existence and ongoing influence (positive and negative) in your life. Consider photos, books, gifts, pieces of clothing, tools, perfumes, things the person has said, events—anything that conjures the person in your mind. Include any plans for the future that you may have that involve the person. Devote at least a sentence or two to each item on your list.

2 ✌ Read through the evidence you have collected as a form of prayer on the person's behalf. Give thanks not only for the influence that the person has had on you but for the person's defining traits and habits—his or her personality and wonderfulness as a creature. Pray your worries for the person. (This is one of my favorite forms of prayer, by the way. I call it "pray-worrying.") Pray your hopes for the person's future, and for your own. Imagine that the person is physically present with you, as you pray, and add whatever you would say to God and to the person if he or she were there.

3 ✌ What have you learned from this experience? Record any revelations.

CHAPTER TWO

Separation Anxiety

If YOU HAVE EVER TRIED to wean a baby from your presence at bedtime, you know that a child isn't born with the understanding that parents still exist after they leave the room or that they will return when Baby wakes up. Regardless of how quickly you respond to any legitimate-sounding cry for comfort (and have been responding ever since Baby was born), he or she startles wide awake and wails inconsolably when you remove your hand from the crib railing or stop humming or, God forbid, take a step in the direction of the door. Sometimes the wailing goes on for weeks of bedtimes! From the baby's point of view, a parent's impending invisibility amounts to abandonment and aloneness, because infants know as real only what they can see and touch and hear and smell and taste. To an infant, what is imperceptible does not exist.

And if, while playing hide-and-seek, you have ever seen children hide their own eyes to make *themselves* invisible, you know that toddlers and sometimes even older children still struggle with the concept of invisibility. Their confusion demonstrates their reasoning:

If I cannot see you, then you cannot see me. You are, in essence, gone, no longer there, even though I may expect to see you when I open my eyes.

Young children, in other words, equate invisibility with absence. They would certainly be crippled by fears if they did not develop, early on in life, a way to deal with the reality that their parents will not always be physically available to them.

Jean Piaget, an early twentieth-century psychologist whose theories remain foundational to this day in the field of child cognitive development, coined the term "object permanence" to describe the understanding, developed in the first years of life, that an object might continue to exist even though it is no longer discernibly present.[1] According to Piaget, who devoted years to observing and recording his own children's behavior from birth onward, the child's struggle to understand the connection between the sensory inner world of the self and the confusing outer world *beyond* the self—much of which might *not* be understood through the senses—begins in earliest infancy. Piaget's conclusions about children's development of a concept of object permanence reveal much about how humans come to believe in an invisible and otherwise imperceptible but omnipresent—and, more importantly, *always* present—God.

The earliest humans, judging from the first few chapters of Genesis, would have had no difficulty grasping the concept that God was always there. The language the Genesis writer uses to describe God's first interactions with humans omits any suggestion of God's invisibility—and omits it so entirely, in fact, that I have always found it hard to believe that God actually *was* invisible and bodiless in those days. God seems to be bodily present in Eden: "Then the man and his wife heard the sound of the LORD God as he was walking in the garden in the cool of the day" (Genesis 3:8). God stood by as the man named the creatures, conversed with the first human couple, and had parental-sounding discussions with their son Cain. God was intimately acquainted with the creatures of Earth from the beginning and was—judging from the Bible's accounts of those early days—a visible, audible, tangible member of their world.

After God drove the first humans out of the Garden, however, and banished Cain to the land of Nod—where, Cain complained, he would be "hidden" from God's presence (Genesis 4:14)—humans became increasingly separated from God. Apparently, God no longer walked among humans, and there were new rules of engagement. Instead of digging contentedly in the lovely garden God had constructed for them, humans would now toil and sweat. People would "die"—that is, they'd either stop existing altogether or else enter an invisible after-existence that could only be guessed at. As the world aged, the divine presence, as represented in scripture, would increasingly be experienced by proxy—angels, prophets, words in scrolls. God as a seeable and hearable and touchable person grows less and less accessible in the course of the Old Testament, and the later biblical writers often complain that God is sleeping or not paying attention, has turned away, or is altogether absent.

Despite God's biblical appearances to certain people and scriptural promises of love and protection; despite the apostle Paul's later assertion that "since the creation of the world God's invisible qualities . . . have been clearly seen, being understood from what has been made" (Romans 1:20); despite the eventual incarnation of God as one of us; humankind has been, since those early days when God walked among them, consumed by separation anxiety. Like babies clutching the crib railing and keening into the darkness, human beings have increasingly felt abandoned by their Creator.

Even Christians, who believe in Jesus as the fleshly embodiment of God, are no better off. For modern readers, the New Testament offers little more than the account of God as a person who *once* lived on earth but is no longer here—was *once* seeable and hearable and touchable, but is no more. Today Jesus is, like his Father, invisible, and he left no artifacts behind—no photograph, no bits of bone, no undisputed image of any kind, not even a description of his face or person—with which we might construct a sense of his physical presence.

Faced with God's material absence from our world, many people —believers, seekers, and unbelievers alike—feel bereft and abandoned at some point in their lives. Even steadfast believers may lose a sense of God's presence temporarily or have doubts about God's existence, not only early on in their faith, like those babies at bedtime, but often late in life, as they near death, the ultimate separation from what may be known through earthly organs of perception.

The Psalms, especially, record humankind's feeling of abandonment and the need for a sense of God's presence and availability in light of this imperceptibility. "Give ear to my words!" the psalmists cry out repeatedly. "Answer me when I call to you, / my righteous God. / Give me relief from my distress; / have mercy on me and hear my prayer" (4:1–2). "Awake, my God!" (7:6). "Why, LORD, do you stand far off? Why do you hide yourself in times of trouble?" (10:1). "How long, LORD? Will you forget me forever? / How long will you hide your face from me? / How long must I wrestle with my thoughts and day after day have sorrow in my heart? . . . Look on me and answer, LORD my God" (13:1–3). To reassure themselves that God, though undetectable, really does exist, the psalmists often name God's qualities and detail past experiences of God. Nevertheless, the Psalms, above all else, give voice to our frustration with God's apparent absence from our world.

One of our most essential spiritual tasks as believers in an invisible God—what Jesus says is the only "work of God" we must perform (John 6:29)—is to believe that, although physically unavailable to us in this world, God really does love us and sent someone to reunite us with our divine parent. Even if we don't sense God near us, faith demands that we believe that God is always present and paying attention. Like the best parent, God hears our complaints, savors our thanks and remorse, and stands ready to attend to our needs.

These are just words, though, to those who have lost or never had a sense of God's presence and to those who feel forsaken or ignored by God in their struggles. When I first came to read the Psalms in the earliest days of my adult faith, the psalmists' affirmations of faith in an attentive and caring God sounded absurd, coming, as these claims invariably did, on the heels of the psalmists' complaints of being unnoticed, not heard, or outright deserted by God.

Consider, for example, Psalm 22, a psalm of David made famous by the fact that its opening lines were on Jesus' lips as he died on the cross. David begins,

> My God, my God, why have you forsaken me?
> Why are you so far from saving me,
> so far from the words of my groaning?
> My God, I cry out by day, but you do not answer,
> by night, but I find no rest. (Psalm 22:1–2)

God is not the only one absent in this psalm. David complains that he is perceived as "a worm, not a human being" and is "scorned by everyone, despised by the people" (Psalm 22:6). His situation gets ever more miserable. He is mocked, insulted, taunted:

"He trusts in the LORD," they say,
"let the LORD rescue him.
Let him deliver him,
since he delights in him." (Psalm 22:8)

David is alone in his distress, apparently abandoned by everyone who loves him and most especially by God, who is not only invisible but seems unwilling to come to David's aid:

Do not be far from me,
for trouble is near
and there is no one to help. (Psalm 22:11)

Still no response, no indication that God has even noticed the psalmist's distress or is anywhere nearby, and David's situation only worsens:

Dogs surround me,
a pack of villains encircles me;
they pierce my hands and my feet.

All my bones are on display;
people stare and gloat over me.

They divide my clothes among them
and cast lots for my garment. (Psalm 22:16–18)

It is hard to imagine circumstances in which one might long more for the confidence of God's presence.

Mysteriously, though, after this catalog of assaults and claims of abandonment—assaults and claims that acquire special poignancy for the modern reader, who knows that they describe the torture and indignities that Jesus will suffer centuries after the psalm was written —David declares,

> You who fear the LORD, praise him!
> All you descendants of Jacob, honor him!
> Revere him,
> all you descendants of Israel!
>
> For he has not despised or scorned
> the suffering of the afflicted one;
> he has not hidden his face from him
> but has listened to his cry for help.
> (Psalm 22:23–24)

Reading the psalmist's words as a new believer, I found David's sudden affirmation of God's abiding and protective presence and the abrupt change of tone from despairing to triumphant utterly baffling. David sounded crazy to me. Even later, after I came to understand the psalm as prophetic foreshadowing of Jesus' future suffering that would result in humankind's long-awaited reunion with their Creator, it was still hard for me to understand the psyche of David, an ordinary believer who likely had no idea that he was speaking about the circumstances of any other sufferer but himself.

Jesus, of course, knew what was happening as he said those words on the cross, I reasoned. *He knew God was at the ready all along. He knew, as he pointed out in the moment of his arrest, that God would put at his disposal "more than twelve legions of angels" to rescue him, if he so desired (Matthew 26:53). He also knew the ultimate outcome of his suffering. Jesus, after all, was God and knew all things.*

But David. How did his faith work? I wondered. *How was he able to affirm God's presence in the very throes of God's apparent absence from the scene of David's agony? How does one convince oneself that God is present and attentive when all sensory evidence demonstrates one's aloneness and abandonment?*

Examination of how babies learn to trust in parents who seem to stop existing the second they leave the room offers some answers to my questions and teaches us much about how we might develop as believers. David's faith is learnable—or, that is, relearnable. Like David, and like the wailing children in cribs we once were, we too might not only seek but affirm the invisible help and comfort available to us from a God who, though imperceptible, stands always at the ready, even when we feel abandoned and alone.

The newborn's perceived world at the moment of birth is a chaos of shapes, colors, smells, sounds, sensations, and movements, few of which carry any meaning. In a matter of days, though, a well cared-for infant is not merely existing in this chaos of perceptions but meaningfully engaging it and even developing expectations about it, as when a newborn mouths the empty air in anticipation of the mother's nipple. This instinctive pursuit of comfort, warmth, and nourishment evolves quickly. The infant explores and learns to differentiate between objects, desiring certain ones above others, and exhibits distress when parents or favored objects disappear from view.

Before long, infants grope after objects held at a distance and even briefly search for objects that have temporarily disappeared. Eventually, having laid aside one object to regard another, the infant will return to the place where the first object was left to look for it. The child repeats these gestures of learning—groping, following an object's movement, returning to where an object had been before— and, through constant experimentation and given lively interaction with a caretaker, gradually builds an understanding of key cognitive rules that govern what cannot be perceived directly. Objects may be hidden, the child learns, or propelled beyond the child's view. A perceived *part* of an object—the fuzzy ear of a partially hidden toy, for example, or its smell or sound—can reveal the presence of the object as a whole. Thus, in early infancy, the child's constant exploration of the visible, known world serves as a pathway to understanding what is invisible or unknown.

Separation anxiety is very observable in this period of development. Baby is becoming more mobile, able to crawl and soon toddle out of the parents' immediate presence, and has yet to learn the most comforting and also most complicated rule governing the perceived world: that objects that disappear entirely—such as parents who leave the room when they put Baby down for an afternoon nap—not only continue to exist but may be trusted to return. By the age of two, most children have developed a mature concept of object permanence. On the basis of known properties of the object, memories of where the object was last seen, and what might be surmised about what such an object is likely to do—such as roll under furniture or reappear in response to noise—the toddler now actively searches for missing things and becomes ever more capable of believing in objects that are physically imperceptible some or all of the time.

Faith in the unseen is clearly foundational to a believer's spiritual progress. The word *faith*, by its very definition, is the ability to believe in something without material evidence. A key biblical definition of faith is "being sure of what we hope for and certain of what we do not see" (Hebrews 11:1). The child's development of the ability to believe in invisible objects is thus analogous to a person's development of faith. In another psalm attributed to David, he argues as much himself:

> I do not concern myself with great matters
> or things too wonderful for me.
>
> But I have calmed myself
> and quieted my ambitions.

I am like a weaned child with its mother;
like a weaned child I am content.
(Psalm 131:1–2)

A child newly weaned from the breast seeks reassurance in the familiar world of the known: a pacifier or a thumb, favorite toys, the
mother's nearness. In this way, they revisit, to use Piaget's way of
describing the maturation process, "visible fractions" of what is lost
as a means of conceptualizing the "invisible whole." Adults suffering
similar separation anxiety in their relationship with God can do the
same.

Consider. As we have seen, God spent intimate time with the first
humans, even standing by—as we stand by our own children, with
the very same excitement—while the man identified the world of the
senses: "Doggie! Horsey! Duck!" After the first couple's expulsion
from the garden, though, God's ongoing companionship and attention, as recorded in scripture, become increasingly less convincing,
and postscriptural experiences of God's physical presence are dramatically less frequent and more indirect.

To counter the loss of God as a real entity in their consciousness, believers over the centuries developed rituals of naming, greeting, and remembering God. They recited litanies, sang songs to
and recorded their experiences of God, memorized scripture, performed the Stations of the Cross, celebrated the Eucharistic meal.
They paced out the territory of their faith through sacramental activities, pilgrimages, public testimonies, and spiritual autobiographies.
Through such exercises of faith, we revisit "visible fractions" of God
as a means of conceptualizing the "invisible whole" of who God is.
The history of Christendom may be understood as an archive of believers' ongoing efforts to substantiate God's imperceptible presence.

In my own period of separation from God, I intuitively—and quite unconsciously—searched for the divine in places where I had sensed God's presence as a child. In churches, mostly empty, that I went out of my way to visit in my travels through Europe and Asia. *To see the art*, I explained to my friends and myself. *To enjoy the architecture of another time. To hear the throb of the organ fill the chilly interior.*

In my Catholic youth, I had sung, a child among old people, in the choir that accompanied the High Mass my parents preferred. Even though I quit the choir in my teens, I still loved the visceral sound of big choral music—Bach's cantatas, Brahms' *A German Requiem*, the Vivaldi *Gloria*, the Masses of Haydn—and listened to it whenever I could. As a high school graduation present to myself, I travelled to England with a friend, and, although my friend wasn't a believer and my own faith was ravaged by then, I forced her to attend evensong— a daily afternoon service of the Anglican church in which local choirboys sing a psalm—in every British town we visited.

Later, when I was teaching in China, by which time God had entirely vanished from my consciousness, a colleague famed for his artistic ability offered to make me a calligraphy scroll. He asked me to give him some poem or quotation I would like him to translate and paint on the scroll, and—although I was a scholar and lover of literature and had never really read the Bible except as a child—the only thing I could think of to give him were two verses from my Mormon neighbors' King James Bible: "Bow down thine ear, O LORD, hear me: for I am poor and needy" (Psalm 86:1) and "Naked came I out of my mother's womb, and naked shall I return thither" (Job 1:21).

I married a devoted Christian, and, though it would be years before I became a believer myself, some of my husband's favorite memories from our early marriage are of me, lying in our bed, reading his Bible. In these and many other ways I unconsciously revisited, again and again, visible fractions of the God I had once known, eventually discovering, when I dropped my hands from my eyes, that God was still there and had been there all along.

It's astonishing, and somewhat discouraging, to consider how frequently biblical writers and the people they write of question where God is in hours of need. Like many famous believers since those times—such as, recently, Mother Teresa of Calcutta—biblical believers sometimes endured long periods when they didn't sense God's presence at all. There is some suggestion in scripture that God may, in fact, turn away on occasion—typically in response to human wrongdoing—and, in many biblical stories, believers flee God themselves and subsequently feel abandoned, the way toddlers feel abandoned when they have wandered off from a parent. It is tempting to interpret a believer's sense of God's absence solely as the result of God's actual abandonment or our flight—that is, as a consequence of sin. And many do. However, Jesus himself, though sinless, clearly experienced some degree of the same forsakenness that people from biblical times to today experience most or even all of the time. Mocked and suffering on the cross, he cried out, in Aramaic, the opening lines of David's agonized psalm: *"Eli, Eli, lema sabachthani?"*—that is, "My God, my God, why have you forsaken me?" (Matthew 27:46). His cry resonates with most believers at some moment in life.

The great desire of believers and would-be believers (and perhaps, secretly, even of confirmed nonbelievers, somewhere behind their closed eyelids or their devotion to an alternative philosophy) is to feel connected to the source of their existence. But often even dedicated believers simply don't. God's physical imperceptibility is a key impediment to our sense of our God's abiding presence, but the church rarely acknowledges God's physical unavailability to us as a problem of faith or offers advice on how to solve it. We call God a person—three persons in one!—and yet we are seemingly on our own in figuring out how to locate this person, or these persons, in our sensory world. It cheers me to reflect that, in infancy, we automatically equipped ourselves—indeed, it seems built into us to do so—with a sophisticated method of solving the problem. Faced with God's seeming absence or abandonment later in life, all we have to do is return to the methods of discovery by which we developed our understanding of the unseen as children.

In an amusing example from his own life,[2] Piaget demonstrates that adults frequently return to the child's patterns of object concept development in searching for lost things. He writes that he often misplaced his "clothes brush," an essential object he apparently made regular use of and kept in a small bag in a special place. Whenever he lost it, he found himself utterly perplexed. I have seen my daughters and husband in the same state of bewilderment many times. My daughters are immediately certain that whatever is missing has been stolen or intentionally hidden—they routinely accuse me of these crimes—and is thus gone forever, or at least until I rediscover it where they left it, in the mess of other lost objects in their rooms or elsewhere in the house.

Piaget, lacking my assistance, mechanically resorts to the same practices that led him to understand the invisible properties of objects in the first place: repeated exploration of what he knew about them to discover a way back to them. He searches for his clothes brush in the places where he has last seen it or where his past searches were successful. Like a small child, he returns, in other words, to what he knows, remembers, and may surmise about the invisible object. Similarly, faith in an invisible God entails systematically returning to what we know, remember, and may surmise about God from our own experience.

1 ❧ In his first year as Pope, Benedict XVI responded to a child's complaint that she couldn't *see* God by explaining that there are many things people easily believe in that they can't see, such as reason, intelligence, souls, and electricity. In fact, he explained, "we do not see the very deepest things, those that really sustain life and the world, but we can see and feel their effects," and he went on to cite one such sustaining force as "the Risen Lord."[3] What other invisible but obviously real things might you add to Pope Benedict's list? What are some important things you believe in that are imperceptible to the senses?

2 ❧ Consider an event in your life that seemed to evidence the existence of something beyond the sensory world as you know it. It may have been a sense of God's presence, or it may have been something else, something you sensed was evil or frightening. Perhaps it was a vision or a seemingly prophetic dream or some other otherworldly experience. What sorts of sensory or conceptual evidence made you feel it was real?

3 ❧ Although I had never before had skin trouble, I once developed an embarrassing and painful case of acne all over my neck and face after a display of arrogance on my part that got me in trouble and made me ashamed of myself. I was a new believer at the time, and I was sure the acne came in response to my arrogance. Of course, any doctor would say that if there were a connection between my acne and the display of arrogance at all, it was that stress caused the acne. Consider a perplexing occurrence in your life and try to read it as experiential evidence of God's loving interaction with you. Might God have been guiding, warning, protecting, affirming, chiding, or punishing you?

4 ❧ Recall an experience, like Piaget's, of not being able to find something in a place where you were sure you had left it. What steps did you instinctively take to find it? Make a list of them. Now consider someone you have not heard from in many years—a long lost classmate or colleague, perhaps, or childhood friend. Without using an Internet person-finder, how might you go about relocating that person? Make another list. Study your two lists of recovery efforts. Are they the same? Do they share certain strategies? Think creatively about what your lists might reveal about your usual way of locating things and people whom you've lost track of and have thus become "invisible." Might any of your strategies be used to help you relocate God in your life?

5 ❧ Review your own history for holy moments or instances of when you felt you were in God's presence. Where were you? What were you doing? Which of your senses were involved in the experience: sight, sound, smell? Revisit some of these moments of connection with the divine by returning to those places and activities (or similar ones) and thus re-creating potential moments of connection in your current life.

CHAPTER THREE

The Evidence
of Things Seen

ONE PLEASANT SPRING AFTERNOON, while driving along the road with my daughters, I pointed out the dazzling rays of God's glory streaming down from a pink cloud on the horizon. Charlotte was immediately irked.

"That's *my* idea about the light from the clouds being from God. You're acting like *you* made it up," she complained—ruining, with her crabby remark, not only the potential shared consciousness of God's magnificent presence but the atmosphere in the car for the rest of the drive. She became silent after that and left me to consider, in the silence, the curse of teenage peevishness and, eventually, her claim.

Charlotte was right in attributing the origin of the idea to herself. From her earliest childhood she had interpreted light rays from clouds as clear evidence that God was really there and lamented that she got to witness this natural occurrence and other sure signs of God's company only rarely. What she didn't know—what I had never told her, because I didn't want to cheapen a cherished childhood revelation—was that *many* people sense the presence of God when they see streams of light coming down from clouds. I had never explained to her that, in my own childhood, *I* had interpreted such light in the same way. I had never pointed out that God is more likely to be depicted in an illustration as light coming from a cloud than as an old man draped in white. I had never mentioned that one of the official definitions of the word *glory*—often used to describe God's presence—is a natural phenomenon involving light. Although the phenomenon in question is technically a halo-shaped rainbow, nevertheless if one searches Internet images for "glory," one is sure to encounter numerous amateur photographs featuring light fingers streaming down from clouds.

The very commonness of Charlotte's idea about God's presence being manifested in certain natural displays makes it, for me, especially persuasive. How could Charlotte, as a toddler, have come up with the same notion that I and so many others had also come up with, apparently independently of one another, unless there were some truth behind it? I feel the same way about the abundance of great flood stories in ancient literature, which some cite as proof that the Bible is just another myth. Even in my atheist years, when I had lost all sense of God's presence and all confidence that anything in the Bible was true, I nevertheless thought that so many people from so many cultures all writing of a great flood was a powerful argument that the flood in Genesis must actually have happened.

The idea that God's presence may be experienced in natural phenomena has considerable support in scripture. Biblical prophets and poets routinely tap the natural world to convey the divine. God is light, a branch, fire, a star, a dove, breath, a rock, a hen, a lamb, a vine, water, wind, a sunrise, language, life. God's character is revealed through such metaphors, I would argue, not merely because God and the created world share many traits but because nature really does display who God is, as the psalmist explicitly declares:

The heavens declare the glory of God;
the skies proclaim the work of his hands.

Day after day they pour forth speech;
night after night they display knowledge.

They have no speech, they use no words;
no sound is heard from them.

Yet their voice goes out into all the earth,
their words to the ends of the world. (Psalm 19:1–4)

As we have already seen, the apostle Paul—who never met Jesus in the flesh but only in a vision that occurred long after Jesus had died, risen, and returned to heaven—argued that even those who, like Paul, never actually *saw* God are nonetheless "without excuse" not to believe in God because "since the creation of the world God's invisible qualities—his eternal power and divine nature—have been clearly seen, being understood from what has been made" (Romans 1:20). Paul uses a temporal clause—"since the creation of the world"—that expresses continuance from the past into the present and also the verb forms "have been clearly seen" and "being understood," which reference current seeing and understanding. The physical world, in short, revealed God from its inception and, by its nature, continues to oblige acknowledgment of God's existence and abiding presence.

The writer of the book of Hebrews further connects the invisible world of God with the visible one we experience through our senses:

Now faith is being sure of what we hope for and certain of what we do not see. This is what the ancients were commended for.

> By faith we understand that the universe was formed
> at God's command, so that what is seen was not
> made out of what was visible. (Hebrews 11:1–3)

In other words, not only does the created world serve as evidence that our invisible God exists, but its very essence is, like God, invisible. God created what is seen out of what *isn't* seen—out of what we, relying on our senses, would call "nothing." But our invisible God and the invisible substance out of which we were created, intangible though they are, are by no means "nothing." Without them, our world and we ourselves would not even exist. The material world is, to put it another way, a tangible expression of the immaterial world: the physical manifestation of the invisible qualities of its Creator.

But what are these invisible qualities? How, exactly, are God's eternal power and divine nature exhibited in the created world? To answer that, we must step outside, into nature, and consider it.

People go outside rarely these days, it seems to me. Back when my husband Kris and I farmed full-time, we were out in nature daily, often all day long. Our first and last tasks of the day were to "check the heifers," as we called it, a job that involved first locating our herd of young cows pregnant with their first calves and then walking among them to count them and make sure they were not having trouble calving or somehow escaping into the road or putting their heads through a fence to get at the tasty Johnson grass, which grows in most of the ditches along the road and becomes poisonous in extreme hot or cold temperatures. Checking the heifers often led to some larger outdoor task, like delivering a calf or repairing a hole somewhere along the miles of barbed wire fences enclosing and dividing our pastures. Once we had made sure the heifers were all right, we drove the pickup through the main cow herd to check on them and their calves.

Then we spent the remainder of the day, if there was any of it left, doing whatever was the job of that season: weaning, vaccinating, haying, repairing machinery, breaking ice on the ponds, fixing fences. Back then, we were outside so much that Kris had a permanent hatline, above which his forehead was a startling white in contrast to his dark red-brown face and neck.

Our neighbors were also farmers in those days, and often we would see one in the distance, beyond the boundaries of our land, going about his own seasonal tasks. Sometimes the neighbor would stop by and comment on whatever we were doing or offer to help us if we had a cow out or a piece of machinery broken down in the field. I was brand new to the area in those days and recognized few of these men, but their sun-darkened faces and forearms were copies of Kris's, and they all had, it seemed to me, the same sort of slow kindliness, the same wisdom and good humor. That the farmers I was coming to know—my husband, the neighbors, the people at forage field-days and at the sale-barn where we sold our cattle—were morally superior to everyone else was surely a misperception on my part. Surely these people's simple decency and neighborliness—like what you might encounter in a George Eliot novel or the poems of Robert Frost— were the products of something other than merely being outdoors messing around with plants and animals for a good part of the day. I have known outdoorsy types—surfers, rock climbers, cyclists—who have not impressed me this way. Nevertheless, it seemed to me then, having grown up in suburbia and having had jobs that kept me inside much of the time, that farming made people seem closer to God in their demeanor: humbler, wiser, sweeter.

Nowadays, in any case, most of our neighbors have, like us, abandoned farming, and I never see any of them outside. I took up running a while back, alternating between morning and evening runs on nearby back roads, which are fronted on both sides by our neighbors' farms and houses and landscaped yards. Even on my longest runs of eight or nine miles, I typically see no people at all. *When do they mow their yards?* I marvel as I huff along. *Or collect their mail? Where do their children play?* The only signs of life I notice are wild creatures in abundance—deer, snakes, frogs, and birds and bugs of all kinds— plus the occasional horse or dog and a few small herds of fancier cattle for show.

I don't know when this migration inside happened. Was there some key event that caused people to suddenly disappear from yards and farms and roadsides? Even in the Southern California cul-de-sac of my early youth—a place that I think of nowadays as a hermetic system of interiors: glossy kitchens, carpeted hallways, garages, station wagons—the whole world was outside, in my memory. We kids were in every yard, up on the hill above the houses and the canyon below, playing on seesaws and swing sets and Slip 'n Slides, collecting bugs, making dolls out of ice plant and twigs, peering into the gutter grate at skunks and rattlers. Our mothers stood or sat in chatty clots nearby, diapering the babies, running after an escaped toddler, sunning, plant- ing petunias along the driveway. Our older sisters and brothers appeared in the distance, walking home from school, and they lingered in the sunlight with their lunchboxes to brag or chase us or chat with their friends. Only the fathers were absent—cloistered, in my dad's case, in a cubicle in a city an hour away—but even they were outside on the weekend, push-mowing the strips of lawn, lugging bags of clippings to the street, rearranging the trashcans, barbecuing.

I know this outdoor living wasn't just my experience. My friends tell similar stories of their growing up years. And in films depicting the time of my childhood and earlier, people are outside a lot. What happened between then and now? Is it that virtual reality has increasingly replaced the natural world as a point of focus? Or is it that we all work, and work too much, exiting our garages early in the morning and pressing the button on our garage door openers to sail back in late in the evening, never once having really been out in God's creation? At my university, I go whole days, on occasion, not knowing if it's sunny or overcast outdoors or whether, as my elderly mother-in-law worries, it's windy or sleeting or threatening to "get bad" in some other way. Weeks may pass without my being aware of any plants or animals or other natural phenomena, except for maybe our dogs and my neglected garden. At best, I see the world outside on my rides to and from work, through the protective windows of my car and at a speed of sixty-five miles an hour, in snatches of color and movement I hardly notice as I listen to the radio and grope for my buzzing cell phone and steer.

My point is, how can we witness and understand "God's invisible qualities—his eternal power and divine nature" clearly displayed in "what has been made" if we aren't out in it? How can we sense God's presence in the created world if we spend all of our time in an interior of our own devising—an interior, in most cases, designed to keep us ignorant of the existence of wind and rain and searing or sinking temperatures and thus also blind to everything nature has to show us about God? When we spend all our time indoors, we don't notice what's growing where, what animals are making what sounds, and all the other natural confirmations that God not only exists but stands by, as our mothers did when we were little, to watch over and enjoy us. Unless we enter God's creation, we miss out on considerable evidence that God longs to be noticed by us and to interact directly in our lives. Spending time outside affords us many startling discoveries about God.

The diversity of nature, for example. God could have created just one kind of plant, one kind of mammal, one kind of bird. Instead, God created not only trees and grasses and flowers but thousands of kinds of trees and grasses, millions of flowers. If I researched the numbers—if it were possible to do so with any accuracy—I wouldn't be surprised to find that there are millions or even billions of different trees, trillions of flowers. Plus every manner of mammal and bird. Plus reptiles, fish, insects, and microscopic creatures—and, within even these categories, countless subcategories. Even a single creature invariably differs from others of its type in age, gender, disposition, coloring, behavior, and purpose. Many creatures even change from one being to another—from a caterpillar to a butterfly or a polliwog to a frog—in the course of their existence. Clearly, diversity is a key value of the world's creator. God must like all kinds of plants, all kinds of animals, all kinds of humans, all kinds of dirt. If it were not so, God wouldn't have made all these things in such variety and pronounced them good.

A glance through God's thundering demonstration of power and authority in response to Job's complaints offers a seemingly exhaustive celebration of the sheer diversity of creation—although, in reality, it's *not* exhaustive; it hardly *begins* to catalogue even the major categories of the different living creatures God fashioned out of what is not seen! After forty lines devoted to stars and weather and things of the atmosphere, God catalogues animal upon animal—mountain goats, does and their fawns, donkeys, horses, hawks, and many more—detailing not only the general traits that differentiate one from the next but the peculiar habits that account for the idiosyncratic personality of each. Of ostriches alone, God comments, in the words of the author of Job,

The wings of the ostrich flap joyfully,
though they cannot compare
with the wings and feathers of the stork.

She lays her eggs on the ground
and lets them warm in the sand,

unmindful that a foot may crush them,
that some wild animal may trample them.

She treats her young harshly, as if they were not hers;
she cares not that her labor was in vain,

for God did not endow her with wisdom
or give her a share of good sense.

Yet when she spreads her feathers to run,
she laughs at horse and rider. (Job 39:13–18)

The variety of creation not only demonstrates God's power, creativity, and enthusiasm for difference, but also suggests the variety of the divine relationship with creation. God can "pull in the leviathan with a fishhook" (Job 41:1), enter into an agreement with it, enslave it, force its mouth open, skin it, stand up to it, destroy it, and even "put it on a leash" to make it a household pet (Job 41:5). That God *can* interact in these ways suggests the desire to do so and argues that God's interaction with creation may be as diverse as creation itself.

And that's just diversity. Many of God's other invisible qualities —such as love, holiness, order, rage, mercy, justice, generosity, jealousy, delight—are all demonstrated in the created world, if we're just willing to enter it and pay attention.

1 ✂ Take a tape measure, four long nails, and some string or yarn and go outside. Find a flat grassy or weedy spot and measure out one square foot, driving the nails into the corners and looping the string around the nails to define the space. Now lie down in front of the square and observe it closely. Count the plants and animals you see and examine each one. Watch it for fifteen minutes. If any creature you see moves, describe what it's doing. Make a list of what you discover.

2 ✂ Consider your list as demonstrative of God in some way. What characteristics of God are demonstrated in that one square foot of grass? Record them.

3 ✂ Read Exodus 34:6–7, a self-description of God offered to Moses. What attributes do you find there? List them, even those characteristics and habits—such as punishing—that may not fit your notion of God's nature. Go outside again and look for evidence of these traits in the natural world. Walk around, interact with the created world as much as possible, and observe closely. Use all your senses. Consider not only what you see and hear and smell but what you know about the plants and creatures you encounter. Be creative. Spend at least a half an hour. If possible, repeat the same exercise at night. Record anything you come up with.

CHAPTER FOUR

Inattentional Blindness—

Or, Noticing: The Skill We Lose As We Age

I KEEP TALKING ABOUT paying attention. I wasn't paying attention when my faith left me. Because we can't see or hear God, it seems to us that God is not paying attention to us, when, in reality, we're the ones not paying attention. Paul claims that since the creation of the world God's invisible qualities have been clearly seen, but we may not have been paying attention. To begin to experience God in the created world, we need to go outside and pay attention to what we see. In brief, faith in an invisible God, I have been arguing, entails paying attention to the evidence of God's presence.

I will continue to talk about paying attention in the chapters that follow. In fact, paying attention is so much what this book is about that I was tempted to title it just that: *Paying Attention*. My overall message is that, even if you don't sense God's presence, God is really there; you just need to pay attention.

Just. I hate that word and generally try to avoid it in my writing, speaking, and especially praying. *Father, just* . . . may communicate, to some, the supreme power of God to shoulder burdens and complete tasks we find impossibly heavy or hard. And *just say no* may mean, to some, that doing so is easy, if you *just* have the right priorities. To me, though, the word *just*, of necessity, belittles the task in question. To say, "you *just* need to pay attention," is to present the task as a simple undertaking, something a child can do.

And, indeed, paying attention *is* something children do well. From the moment of birth, babies instinctively pay close attention to what's going on around them—not just the breast or bottle that nourishes them and the warm arms that transport and comfort them, but noises, movement, and all of the visual, gustatory, olfactory, and tangible data that constitute the unknown world into which they are born. Babies notice everything, and noticing teaches them to understand what they are seeing and make things happen and get what they want. Indeed, newborns pay such careful attention that they notice patterns everywhere, subtle keys that enable them, even before they can think in words, to turn raw sensory information into meaning. In the space of just a year or two, babies are able to sort out the noises adults make well enough not merely to reproduce them accurately and parrot them back but to manipulate those noises for their own purposes. No trained teacher or books are involved in this miraculous evolution of an infant into a speaker. The child learns speech, without being taught, entirely through paying attention.

Given young children's early knack for paying attention, given the success inevitably won through their work of noticing what's going on around them, one would think that paying attention would come easily to anyone who was once a child and is now proficient in communication and other functional skills essential to adults. Surely, as a prescription for finding God and remaining aware of God's presence, paying attention is a light burden, an easy task, just as Jesus promises when he says, "my yoke is easy and my burden is light" (Matthew 11:30). Certainly, paying attention is easier than following all the laws in Leviticus or living as a hermit or most other spiritual feats one might invent.

But, you might argue, Jesus isn't talking about locating an apparently absent God in the "easy yoke, light burden" passage. He's talking about leading the Christian life. That's how pastors and commentators typically explain the passage, in any case.

And, if you go to Matthew 11 and examine the passage in context —do!—you'll find that Jesus is *not* talking explicitly about sensing God's invisible presence but rather proposing an antidote—namely, sharing our work with Jesus—to the weary burden of struggling along without God. "Come to me, all you who are weary and burdened, and I will give you rest," he begins. "Take my yoke upon you and learn from me, for I am gentle and humble in heart, and you will find rest for your souls. For my yoke is easy and my burden is light" (Matthew 11:28–30). *Come to me, learn from me, yoke yourself with me,* he says, *and I will pull with you, and "you will find rest for your souls."*

But how do we yoke ourselves to a partner we cannot sense beside us?

Jesus' advice that his listeners yoke themselves to him was part of his response to John the Baptist's doubting query from prison, "Are you the one who was to come, or should we expect someone else?" (Matthew 11:3). After first sending John's disciples back to John to "report what you hear and see: The blind receive sight, the lame walk, those who have leprosy are cleansed, the deaf hear, the dead are raised, and the good news is proclaimed to the poor" (Matthew 11:4–5), Jesus asks the crowd that remained the same question three times: "What did you go out to see?" (Matthew 11:8, 9). His message, both to John and his disciples and to the crowd, is the same. *What are you looking for when you look for evidence of God?* he asks. *It's right there in front of you. Look at it! Listen to it! Pay attention!*

Before going on to make the yoke and the burden comment, Jesus publicly prayed, "I praise you, Father, Lord of heaven and earth, because you have hidden these things from the wise and learned, and revealed them to little children. Yes, Father, for this was your good pleasure" (11:25–26). Then, as Jesus frequently did when praying in public, he transformed the prayer into a sermon directed toward those around him: "All things have been committed to me by my Father. No one knows the Son except the Father, and no one knows the Father except the Son and those to whom the Son chooses to reveal him" (11:27). Jesus' father, he's saying, is not so easy to figure out. *But no worry*, Jesus tells his listeners. *I get him, and, with my help, you can do the same.* It is at this point that Jesus takes up the topic of sharing his yoke and burden. Jesus' real topic in the yoke and burden passage, in summary, is the hiddenness of God. Whereas children have the natural capacity to see God, Jesus argues, adults don't. For adults, God must be revealed.

If my own experience as a child believer is representative of others', children unthinkingly notice God. I noticed God's presence when listening to stirring music, during certain parts of the Mass, while roaming the woods, while picking berries. To discover God, Jesus is telling us, we need to be like little children. He recommends this explicitly elsewhere: "Truly I tell you, anyone who will not receive the kingdom of God like a little child will never enter it" (Mark 10:15). To "receive" God's kingdom as a little child involves nothing more complicated than noticing that it's being offered, accepting the gift, and enjoying it.

Breathe. This is as theologically dense as I'm capable of being. And what I want to argue, here, is actually quite simple: Jesus continually reveals God to us, but, unlike the little children he speaks of, we don't notice. As we mature, we stop paying attention. It seems that the maturation process itself is to blame. Apparently, although babies notice everything and what they notice helps them understand the world and communicate and get what they want, as they grow older, they notice less and less. By adulthood, we notice only what is relevant to our most important occupation in a given moment—and even then only superficially.

Interestingly, artists and scholars have long known that, as we age, we pay less and less attention to what's going on around us. In her drawing primer, *Drawing on the Right Side of the Brain*, art educator Betty Edwards compares drawings made by people at different ages.[1] Younger children, although somewhat hampered by less developed hand-eye coordination, often draw more accurately than older children and adults because young children try to draw what they see, rather than what they think they *should* be seeing. In drawing a human face, for example, young children may reproduce for eyes the short lines or messy triangles they actually see, whereas adolescents and adults are more likely to produce the almond-shaped, eyelash-rimmed symbol for eye, with all the nameable parts—pupil, iris, lid, brow— that they have learned over the years are what constitute eyes. Unless trained to do so, they don't really look at the actual eye they are drawing but only at the preconceived image of an eye in their minds.

Scientists have a name for our inability to see what's right in front of us: namely, "inattentional blindness." We perceive very little of all the potential input we could be perceiving at any given moment because we're only paying attention to a tiny fraction of it—the part that pertains to *us* in the moment of perception, during which time we are occupied with a given task or goal. What we see reflects what we care about—that is, what we're paying attention to—and what we *expect* to see. Taken together, what we care about and what we expect to see amount to a very small portion of what's actually there.

It is difficult to see what we are not expecting. Witnesses and even victims of crimes routinely err in their reports, even when their accounts are collected just minutes after a crime occurs. They don't notice the details *as* the crime is happening, because it's only *after* the crime has occurred that the details become important and they have a reason to start paying attention. In a famous study of inattentional blindness called *Gorillas in Our Midst*,[2] visual cognition scholars Daniel J. Simons and Christopher F. Chabris asked subjects to watch a video of a ballgame and count how many times the ball was passed by one of the teams. The video was rigged with a glaring distraction: A woman dressed as a gorilla walked out into the middle of the game, faced the camera, pounded her chest, then exited. A surprising fifty percent of the viewers, Simons and Chabris found, did not notice her. They were concentrating on the game itself, trying to see those passes as well as they could and noticing little else, no matter how surprising. They saw primarily what they expected to see.

Indeed, according to animal scientist Temple Grandin, *"Humans are built to see what they're expecting to see."*[3] Grandin visits the topic of inattentional blindness in her book *Animals in Translation: Using the Mysteries of Autism to Decode Animal Behavior*. A common trait of people who are autistic is the lack of a sensory filter that sorts perceptions into relevant and irrelevant categories. As a result of this lack, autistic people—and animals, according to Grandin—tend to notice pretty much everything, very intensely and all at the same time, whereas nonautistic people typically notice only what is relevant to them, which is primarily what they are setting out to notice in a given situation. Grandin, who is autistic herself, argues that seeing what one expects to see is an important human faculty that helps humans plan for possible dangers. Inattentional blindness, in other words, is a survival skill that helps people maintain control over their environment. But, as its scientific name suggests, it can also be a handicap that hinders us from seeing what we don't expect. As Grandin comments, "it's hard to *expect* to see something you've never seen."[4] Such as evidence of the invisible God in our midst, for example.

Little children see more of what's going on around them than adults do—and are thus better at perceiving God than adults are, I would argue—because seeing and hearing and tasting and smelling and feeling the world in order to make sense of it is their primary task. As future participants in the chaos into which they were born, they are in the business of collecting information and ordering it. They are only beginning to solidify an understanding of how the perceived world is likely to work, only just learning the focus on the predictable that will ensure their survival in the knowable world. To a small child, anything is possible, everything is a miracle, and our invisible Creator is manifest in the very nature of creation, just as Paul says. Witness my daughter Charlotte's and my baby enthusiasm for rays of light streaming from clouds and our shared conviction, from earliest childhood, that those rays emanate from the Creator directly. As children mature, though, they increasingly sort and organize what they perceive into usable knowledge and reject or ignore anything that interferes with or contradicts what they have thus far learned of how things are likely to work. The older they become, the less receptive they are to evidence of the surprising spiritual world behind the knowable reality they have constructed. They become, increasingly, blind to God.

It is tempting to take these speculations—and that's what they are, on my part—much further. Blindness is a major theme of Jesus' teaching, after all, and God's habits of self-disclosure are complex.

Does God miraculously and single-handedly heal believers' spiritual blindness when they come to faith, or do they learn a new way of seeing? Or is it, as I believe, some combination of God's sovereign power and our seeking that leads to a sense of God's presence? When asked what work God expects of people, Jesus answered, "The work of God is this: to believe in the one he has sent" (John 6:29). Read this equation in reverse, and you get that believing in God—that is, accepting God's invisible presence as real—is "work." A task to be undertaken. A sense of God's presence is not something we should just sit around and wait for or complain isn't there. We have to go find it.

It is tempting, as I say, to examine our increasing inattention to God in relation to scarier questions about works, such as whether spiritual blindness constitutes an active rejection of God. I will leave such questions to professional theologians. Let me just add, though, that I have participated in many conversations with fellow faculty and administrators at my university about what I would argue is a form of inattentional blindness we routinely encounter in Christian higher education. New students often arrive so convinced of whatever brand of faith they were raised in that they seem disinclined and sometimes even incapable of learning anything *new*. They are, in other words, so exclusively focused on what they already know, or think they know, that they can't see anything else and are thus limited in their capacity to grow, both intellectually and spiritually. Many shut down and become angry whenever they encounter anything that challenges their existing views, and, since it is the business of universities to teach new information and help students learn, such students are shut down and angry much of the time. We refer to them as "foreclosed"—closed, in advance of their arrival in our classes, to much of what we are trying to teach about God through our various scholarly disciplines. Interested, as we faculty are, in their spiritual formation as well as their success in our courses, we try to devise ways to get them to open up to the possibility that God may not look and act as they have imagined or been taught elsewhere, but it is like trying to make toddlers taste food they have decided, in advance, is utterly noxious: They squeeze mouths and eyes shut and may even cover their ears to avoid it.

God willing, such foreclosed students will open up over time. Others will leave us in outrage. Some, just as Jacob wrestled with the angel, will continue to wrestle with us until they receive a blessing, and some may falter in their faith for a long time and perhaps decide that God must not exist at all, only to rediscover God, as I did, after many years of loneliness and longing. Far be it from me to judge God's ways of drawing us closer. The Jacobs of the world—and I have been one of them—will wrestle their way into God's presence, no matter what I say here. But a far simpler and usually less painful way of learning to recognize God is to emulate little children, who are natural learners, and relearn their primary learning strategy, which is to notice everything they can in the sensory repository of truth in which they find themselves. To enter God's kingdom as a little child, as Jesus recommends, is to learn to pay attention. To collect and savor the sight and sound and smell and taste and feel of God's kingdom. To expect to be surprised.

But, as Grandin points out, "it's hard to *expect* to see something you've never seen." Perhaps impossible. Especially if you know in advance that the thing is invisible.

Once, as an alternative certification requirement for teaching grades seven through twelve at my local school, I took an introductory course in special education. It was one of the most interesting and useful courses I ever took, although in all my years of teaching I only ever had two or three students with the sorts of special needs we studied. The professor clearly loved students with special needs and thus made the prospect of working with such students in our classes exciting. For him, every learning disability was a pedagogical riddle and a delight. Once, at a formal dinner, he coached a group of blind college students to envision the position of the hands of a clock at different times in order to locate different dishes on their plates so they could eat with dignity. "Your mashed potatoes are at two o'clock," he'd whisper. On another occasion, he had watched an autistic student cross a classroom diagonally by stepping up and over every desk in his way. The child wasn't being intentionally disruptive, the professor explained. Rather, he knew where he wanted to go and was taking the most direct route there. It never occurred to the boy that there might be a more expedient way to get where he was going, such as following the perimeter of the room or passing between the desks. Helping that boy learn amounted to helping him envision and consider alternative behaviors before acting. The professor gave lots of examples of the candor of developmentally disabled children, whom he summed up as "on the mind, out the mouth," which made me feel a special affinity to them. I could listen to that professor tell his stories forever.

I learned several new pedagogical ideas in that class. 1) To teach a person with special needs, you need to first study the task at hand and learn its problematic features. 2) Difficult tasks are more learnable if you break them down into doable portions and then practice those portions individually before reassembling them into a cohesive whole. 3) *Every* person has, in some sense, special needs. These educational concepts may sound like truisms, but they have transformed my teaching since that time and merged into what has become my teaching—and learning—philosophy in all subjects, at all levels. No matter how smart and gifted you are, to learn how to do something new, you must first examine it, then break it down into manageable portions, then practice it.

Paying attention to God's presence, as I have said, is probably more difficult than it might seem. We may set out to pay attention, as those did who watched the ballgame and counted passes, but entirely miss the gorilla in our midst. It is likely to be hard, as Grandin says, to *expect* to see—or hear or feel—someone whom we have not only never seen before but whom we know to be unseeable, unhearable, and intangible.

That, then, is the first portion that the task of paying attention to God's presence must be broken into: to accept—that is, to understand and believe—that, although God is imperceptible, God's presence *may* be discerned. To locate God in our lives, in other words, we must learn first to be "sure of what we hope for," as the writer of Hebrews puts it, "and certain of what we do not see" (11:1). We must first *hope* God's presence into faith, as it were.

The next part of the task of paying attention to God, as I see it, is to expect the unexpected. Expect surprises. Expect to find out things about who God is that you didn't know before and even things that contradict what you thought you knew. Open yourself to learning something new.

If you've ever tried to keep yourself from flinching at the scary parts of a horror movie—even a horror movie you've seen many times before—then you know how difficult it is to expect the unexpected. Victims of rape and other assaults by strangers often report afterward that they sensed beforehand that something bad was about to happen, but they didn't take any action to avoid it. Though alert to clues that something wasn't as it should be, they just didn't believe that such an unexpected thing as an attack by a stranger could actually happen. Self-defense courses combat this inability to respond to the unexpected—not so much inattentional blindness, in this case, as willful eye-shutting—by teaching students to plan for unexpected dangers. *Look for the man lurking near your car in the parking lot*, they advise. *Remind yourself that you are prone to ignore danger or explain it away with some rational explanation. Your urge will be to think the man's presence near your car is a coincidence, to concoct some logical reason for why he lingers, to reject the evidence of the unexpected.* Self-defense programs will teach you to embrace the evidence. To ignore your urge to explain it away. They will teach you to preempt it.

"Pay attention to your fear," the instructor will counsel. "Have your keys between your fingers. Envision the potential attacker's weak spots—the groin, the eyes—in your mind. Better yet, leave the scene and go somewhere safe."

Learning to expect the perceptible presence of someone whom you know to be invisible and supernatural amounts to the same sort of undertaking, but hopeful rather than dire. Finding God in our lives demands that we resist the urge to ignore or deny the evidence of what is not seen, the urge to explain away miracles and view God's constant communications as mere coincidences, and instead expect the unexpected.

There is a passage in Paul's letter to the Philippians that I have had wielded at me so many times from so many different directions that I have come to hate it, even though I'm convinced Paul did not mean it the way that most people seem to understand it. "Finally, brothers and sisters," he writes, "whatever is true, whatever is noble, whatever is right, whatever is pure, whatever is lovely, whatever is admirable—if anything is excellent or praiseworthy—think about such things" (4:8). Translated into what people are actually trying to tell me when they quote this verse, it means, "Don't use foul language; don't assign books that have foul language or sex or any other similarly unsavory or unchristian material in them; and for God's sake don't elaborate about your own past or present sins." (You can get a glimpse of my unmentionable life of sin from this analysis, I'm sure.)

People who brandish this passage typically ignore the first item in the series—"whatever is true"—in favor of whatever is noble and pure and, to their minds, lovely. They also neglect to tell me what Paul recommends I do with all this nice thinking: namely, "Whatever you have learned or received or heard from me, or seen in me—put it into practice" (4:9). And they always omit what Paul says will be the result of paying attention to the true, noble, pure, lovely, admirable, excellent, and praiseworthy things in one's vicinity, which is that "the God of peace will be with you" (4:9). *Not*, mind you, that the *peace of God* will be with you. Rather, the promise is that paying attention to the abundant evidence of God's invisible nature will conjure the very person of God. We will enjoy the company of the God of peace. Our frantic searching will end.

Having got my rant out about Philippians 4:8, I am just now feeling more kindly toward the passage than I usually do—impressed, even, with Paul's theological acumen. Nevertheless, even though for some of you I will be violating an important commandment in what I am about to do—don't change or add to the word of God—I would like to retool Paul's words to the Philippians in the interest of unpacking its advice about pursuing the presence of our invisible Creator. "Finally, brothers and sisters," I would have Paul conclude his letter to the Philippians, "whatever is new, whatever is strange, whatever is miraculous, whatever simply cannot be—if anything happens that takes you by surprise or that so contradicts what you already think about God that your every urge is to reject it outright—think about such things. Search out apparent impossibilities and contradictions. Study them. And if you learn or discover or receive in the process any knowledge of God that you didn't have before—put it into practice. And I promise you—if the promise of a one-time atheist and habitual cynic means anything to you—that God will be with you, attentive, engaged, and utterly available. And you will be at peace."

The last part of the task of sensing God's presence—being at peace—is the hardest, I think. Maybe, in this world, it is impossible. Having convinced yourself that your imperceptible Creator *can* be experienced and having located surprising clues of God's ongoing involvement in our world, you must now resist any urges you might have to deny these proofs and, instead, allow yourself to recognize God's presence and be at peace.

Think of it like identifying a bird you have seen in a field guide. First you have to find the right field guide, one for your part of the world. Then you must consider the peculiar characteristics of the bird you saw. It was a smallish bird, say, reddish brown. It latched onto the trunk of the tree sideways, like a woodpecker, instead of perching on a branch. It had a longish, black, woodpecker-like beak. Perhaps it *was* a woodpecker, you guess, and you start with these details, these speculations. But you don't find the bird in your book. Your research does take you to sapsuckers, piculets, and flickers, though—birds that you previously didn't know existed—and you feel you are getting closer. You recall what time of day you saw the bird and where, and you consider what those details might reveal about its habits. You consult other field guides—more comprehensive ones and guides that cover larger areas, areas outside of what you might expect to encounter in eastern Oklahoma, where you live. You seek out and confer with local birdwatchers. With each new discovery, each new clue, you think you are closer to knowing, but no one reports exactly the details you describe. No book features a picture that depicts, categorically, the bird you saw. You return to where you saw the bird and listen for its voice. You look for telling holes in the trunk of the tree on which you think you saw it that first time, but you see none. It is too high up. And perhaps it was a different tree. You think you see the bird again, and you notice more details about it. Its head is lighter than its body. When it flies, it flaps its wings twice, then stows its large, dark feet against its body and spears through the air like something aimed. You have never examined a bird so attentively before.

I have, to be honest, never found that bird in any book, although God knows I've looked. Despite my consultations and research, I've never managed to identify it to my satisfaction. But I have been on the verge of finding the name scientists have given it. I am sure of that. Having considered and researched its characteristics, I know it far better than I did at first, far better than I have known any other bird. And I have seen it now several times. I can recognize it from a distance—its color, its cough of a voice, its spearlike flight. My quest to know that bird has taken me out of the virtually birdless world I knew before and into its realm. And, even if I never identify it to my satisfaction, seeking its name has introduced me, on several occasions, to a peace I didn't even know I lacked.

———————————

I ❧ Paying attention to God, like any other skill, takes practice. To get better at paying attention to God, first practice noticing things in general. Give yourself the assignment of noticing a specific element of the world you encounter daily:

for example, people's eyes or ambient noise or words or clothing. Keep a running list in which you name and describe each item. Do this for a week.

2 ∽ Think of a task you have done so often that you do it without really thinking about it, such as washing clothes or making a certain meal or planting seeds in your garden. Now, find a child or someone who has never done that task before and teach him or her how to do it. Before you start your instruction, carefully consider the following questions: Are there any foundational skills—such as how to sort clothes for washing or use your stove—that you must teach before you begin? Are there any preparations that must be made before starting? What steps would you break the task into? What activities can you devise for your student to practice each of the steps? What order must the steps follow?

3 ∽ If you have been a believer for a long time, consider some God-related task—such as worshipping, offering thanksgiving, or confessing—that you practice or have practiced on a regular basis. Imagine explaining it to someone else who has never done that spiritual activity before and doesn't know how to go about it. What preparations do you need to make before you begin? What steps might that task be broken down into? Do they go in a certain order? What activities might help the person practice those steps?

4 ∽ In the book of Deuteronomy, Moses tells the Israelites, "These commandments that I give you today are to be on your hearts. Impress them on your children. Talk about them when

you sit at home and when you walk along the road, when you lie down and when you get up. Tie them as symbols on your hands and bind them on your foreheads. Write them on the doorframes of your houses and on your gates" (6:6–9). In essence, Moses was giving his people tips on how to keep God's word in their minds. The same methods might be used for nudging us into noticing evidence of God's presence on an ongoing basis.

a ❦ Getting up and lying down: Intentionally reflect on a given topic (it can be anything) when you get up and when you lie down, for a week.

b ❦ Once, when I struggled with an inability to say no in the aftermath of a crime, my friend taught me an unassailable response to say: "No, that simply won't do." The problem was, I couldn't seem to remember the words when I needed them, so I got in the habit by writing the sentence on the palm of my hand. Write a message to yourself that reminds you to pay attention to God in your life and keep it somewhere handy.

c ❦ On the wall in my kitchen, my husband and I keep a running record of the girls' and our heights and the date. Use a similar method to keep track of what you notice about God—not on a wall, necessarily, but in some common area that you are likely to notice when you do certain activities.

CHAPTER FIVE

Scriptural Evidence of God's Presence, Part 1:

What, Exactly, Is the Bible?

*S*UPPOSE, FOR A MOMENT, that you were an only child raised by your mother. She was a sad, reclusive woman—an only child herself, both parents long since deceased—and you led a lonely life growing up. Your father disappeared before you were aware enough to notice, and, since everyone you ever knew had some sort of father, you have always felt the lack of one. For as long as you can remember, you have felt abandoned.

When you were still little, you asked your mother questions about your father, and she told you that he had never really existed to begin with—or, at least, not in the usual understanding. That is, she never knew him. You were, she said, the product of a medical procedure—when you were older you learned to call it artificial insemination—that she underwent in despair of ever finding a mate. She was clearly uncomfortable talking about the matter. She evaded giving details, her language was vague, and she wouldn't look you in the eye. It was almost as if she were lying. When you reported what she had told you to your friends at school, they were astonished and a little unbelieving, and you yourself struggled to accept the story. Why would your mother have done such a thing? But why would your mother tell you that story unless it was true?

In adolescence, your doubts grew. By then your mother patently refused to talk about your conception or birth.

"You know all there is to tell," she said when you asked.

Although you grew used to believing that what she had told you as a child really was how you came to be, every once in a while uncertainty nagged you. Your birth certificate—which you needed to get your driver's license—listed a father's name and gave no indication of any unusual circumstances when you were born. A formality, according to your mother. The nurses had insisted she name a father, so she made one up. Again you sensed that she was hiding something, and you searched your house for evidence of an actual father who once existed. But you found nothing. No photographs of a man who might be your father. No documentation of medical procedures or an adoption or anything else.

After you graduate from college, you marry, and soon you and your spouse are expecting a child of your own. Not long after the baby is born, your mother gets cancer and dies. A few years later, you receive in the mail a heavy carton of papers. In it are letters of all kinds. Most of the letters are to a man whose name was the same as that on your birth certificate. Some are signed with your mother's first name and written in what looks like a younger version of her handwriting. There are also various elementary and high school report cards. There's a padlocked diary decorated in a Pooh Bear theme, written by what sounds like a young girl. There are also several coverless journals written by someone older—and probably male, judging from the kinds of things he talks about: baseball, astronomy, a job cutting neighbors' lawns. There are high school yearbooks, graded papers written for various college courses, the instruction manual for a car, numerous receipts and bills of sale for various items, yellowed articles cut from a small-town newspaper on a variety of topics, and a death certificate for the man on your own birth certificate. In an envelope buried at the bottom of the box, you find pictures of a baby in the arms of a woman in a hospital bed who looks like your mother, only younger than you ever knew her. And happier. In one of the pictures, a man stands beside the bed, and both of them are beaming. Of course the man looks like you.

Whoever sent you these artifacts of your father's existence took pains to remove or distort information crucial for any identification beyond the man's name. Dates are obscured, and the names of people and places, addresses, and certain clumps of words are cut out. Covers and envelopes are missing. There's no return address on the carton, and the postmark is too smudged to read.

Clearly, you aren't ever going to meet your dad. He's dead. But you'd still like to know who he was—what sort of person you'd missed your whole life and what his life might reveal about your mother, what it might reveal about you. Was the man a nice guy or a creep? Where did he live? What did he do for a living? Did he leave behind any other children, your siblings or half-siblings? Is there a wife still living? Brothers or sisters or parents of his who would be the aunts and uncles and grandparents you never had? Nieces and nephews who'd be your cousins? How was your father like you? How was he different?

With a first-rate private investigator and unlimited financial resources and time to spend on research, you fantasize, you might still be able make some educated guesses about your father's identity and former whereabouts. But you don't even know where to begin to locate such an investigator, and you don't have much money. And, you don't have time. You and your spouse both work, and when you're not working you're busy with other things—household chores, raising your children, trying to find time to relax.

Still, there's the box of papers. A miscellany of disparate documents comprising a life story of sorts. The papers hold major keys to who your parents were and who you are now. Written by different people, for different purposes, connected only in that they all reveal some aspect of the unknown man's relationship to others, they nevertheless evidence the actual existence of a father you never knew.

Consider, for a moment, how you would go about reading and rereading the contents of that box. With what frustration and confusion. With what desire to know. With what longing.

That box of papers is pretty much what the Bible was for me when I first started really reading it: an anthology of writings documenting the existence of a God I knew little about as perceived by a bunch of people I had never met. I wasn't a believer yet. I had married a Christian who read the Bible regularly. Kris and I were both readers, so of course I wanted to read what he was always reading. I also wanted to understand his faith. Secretly, I longed to share it. To know the God he claimed not only as Creator and Rule Giver but as his *Father*—someone intimately related to him, someone who knew about him before he was born, who had loved his mother, who had held him in his arms as a baby, who had wanted him in the first place and was glad he existed. I wanted to know the Father Kris knew, to feel what he felt.

Truth be told—and this is a truth we Christians don't like to tell—we know pathetically little about the Bible. Many books of the Bible were anonymously written, and, of those that weren't, scholars have little or no biographical information about the authors. We often have to surmise the writers' purposes in writing, and the writings often address historical events that historians know next to nothing about: trivial wars and disasters, family stories, land purchases, construction projects for buildings no longer in existence—the misfortunes and dreams of people long forgotten.

The writings collected in the Bible include everything from literary works—songs, poems, and stories—to genealogies, censuses, and historical records. Much of the historical material lacks contextual details crucial for corroboration with other historical sources. The Bible is frequently all the history we have about the people and events it documents. Even the literary material poses special challenges. We don't know how to play the music of the Psalms, although the psalmists often provide information about the melody and instruments. The Bible's many poems often employ elaborate literary devices—such as beginning each line with a letter of the Hebrew alphabet and other acrostic schemes or shaping the lines to resemble a Babylonian ziggurat—that are invariably lost in translation. Scholars and believers dispute whether certain biblical stories are parables—and thus fictional and metaphorically intended—or actual accounts. We don't even know, exactly, how these writings came to *be* the Bible as we know it—how the disparate portions came to be collected as the single document we call "the Bible," which simply means "the Book."

Indeed, believers often speak of the Bible as though humans were not involved in its composition at all. As though it were not the product of several centuries of telling, recording, and assembling but were instead an integral document penned by Almighty God—the original ghostwriter, so to speak, writing under a number of pseudonyms. Students in my composition courses at the Christian university where I teach English routinely lead in quotations from biblical sources with the words, "The Bible says . . ."

"No," I tell them. "The Bible can't speak or write. But someone *did* write those words. Who was it?"

Most students have no idea, and I show them how to find out what can be known of this information and how to articulate its relevance for a general audience—that is, for an audience of strangers likely to include people who have never read or studied the Bible. Typically, my students are astonished to realize how much of the Bible is written by unknowns, whom they would need to refer to as something like "the psalmist" or "the author of the book of Hebrews."

Formal documentation of biblical sources has long since been codified in style guides to omit the ancient writers' individual names, but, before I teach my students that, I always make them tell me how a book of the Bible would have to be documented on a *Works Cited* page if it were in any other anthology. The first words of the entry would be the author, they say, but the mere thought of listing *Solomon* or *Paul* as the author of one of the books of the Bible makes them uncomfortable. They also don't want to use *Anonymous*.

"God is the author," someone invariably pipes up.

"Well, then, shall we use *God*?" I prod, and they all laugh uneasily.

Some think I'm being irreverent. Or else that I don't believe that the Bible really is "God-breathed," as Paul describes it (2 Timothy 3:16).

"I do," I reassure them. "But it's also a text of complicated and ancient authorship, and it has all the problems that go along with that. If you want to use the Bible at all as a scholarly source, you'll need to address at least some of these issues."

Believers and nonbelievers alike can be sure of one thing about the Bible: The people who wrote it—as well as the faithful they wrote about—believed in the real presence of God. That's clear from the earnest tone of their stories and from what they say about God. Sometimes biblical authors recount events that they could not have personally witnessed—such as the Creation or the Flood or the Temptation of Jesus—but that they must know either from handed down stories or from some special sort of memory miraculously imparted to their consciousness. Nevertheless, their enthusiasm and confidence as well as the stories themselves argue for an interactive, caring God whose presence is perceptible and cherished.

From the very first pages of scripture, the biblical writers describe a God who worries about the humans' aloneness and who routinely promises to remain with them. Indeed, companionship—or with-us-ness—seems to be one of God's key characteristics.

And humans were made in the image of God. This detail of our conception is so exciting that the writer of Genesis bursts out of prose into song for the first time in scripture when telling of it:

> So God created human beings in his own image,
> in the image of God he created them;
> male and female he created them. (1:27)

That we were created in God's own image is itself an argument for God's presence—or, in any case, an argument that, if *we* want to be with *God*, then *God* also wants to be with *us*. To say it another way, wanting to be *with* the ones we love is likely a trait we have inherited from our Creator.

When the first humans, ashamed of their sin, snuck out of God's presence, God asked—plaintively, it seems to me—"Where are you?" In subsequent biblical accounts, humans' absence from God is typically an indication that things are not right. In fact, sin is pretty much synonymous with leaving God's presence, and God's resulting absence is sin's inevitable, and unbearable, consequence. As Cain laments when God banishes him for killing his brother, "My punishment is more than I can bear. Today you are driving me from the land, and I will be hidden from your presence" (Genesis 4:13). God responds to Cain's worry as any loving parent would when a child leaves home: by taking measures to protect him from harm.

Throughout the Bible, God seems to value human companionship, organizing meeting places with the Israelites—in the desert, at Mount Sinai, in "the land where I am bringing you to live" (Leviticus 20:22)—and reassuring Moses, "My Presence will go with you" (Exodus 33:14). Through Isaiah, God promises a savior called Immanuel, or, as Matthew translates, "God with us" (Isaiah 7:14 and Matthew 1:23). And God counters Jeremiah's grim prophesies of God's wrath toward sinners with this promise: "You will seek me and find me when you seek me with all your heart. I will be found by you" (Jeremiah 29:13–14). In the voices of the biblical writers, we find, if we look for it, a God who is not only present to believers but who also desires *their* presence!

Like us, though, the biblical writers and those in the events they describe were often frustrated in their efforts to sense God's attentive presence. "Where are you?" they wail throughout the Old Testament. But even their despairing questions evidence faith in God's attendance in their lives. Not sensing God's presence, they nevertheless expect it, ardently seek it, and—in account after account, poem after poem, story after story—eventually find it.

Their success, I believe, lies not only in God's promise that those who *want* to find God *will* find God but in the act of seeking itself. To seek God's presence is to anticipate it and thus be alert to the evidence that God is there. As the prophet Micah puts it,

But as for me, I watch in hope for the LORD,
I wait for God my Savior;
my God will hear me. (Micah 7:7)

To seek God, we need to watch in hope, and we will be rewarded with evidence of God's listening presence.

Scripture is full of this evidence, but if you aren't actively seeking it, you may not notice it. The biblical writers not only claim God's presence; they describe it. The people in the events they recount experience God's presence in a multitude of ways: as a companion walking in the garden, as a conversational partner, as a voice speaking from a burning bush, as a pillar of light, as a vision, as a dream, as an angel calling from heaven or a donkey braying, as God's own voice calling to them in the night—"Samuel! Samuel!" (1 Samuel 3:10)—and so on. Even the genealogies offer evidence of God's presence. Nestled in the now meaningless jumble of names are revelations like this one: "Enoch walked faithfully with God; then he was no more, because God took him away" (Genesis 5:24).

In one of my favorite instances of God's presence in scripture, Jacob is traveling and wakes up one night with the thought, "Surely the LORD is in this place, and I was not aware of it" (Genesis 28:16). I've had a similar experience. Once, in a worried period when I was waking in the night a lot, I opened my eyes and, sensing God's presence, thought, "Oh! You're up too." That's how it is more often than not, I suspect. God's up and paying attention. But I'm often not. Just as Micah watches in hope for God's notice, God waits in hope for ours. And the Bible provides example after example of how our mutual longing for each other's presence and attention plays out.

All this is to say that one way of locating or relocating in your own world a seemingly absent God is to read the Bible expressly for evidence of *others'* experiences of God's presence. The results of such a search may initially *add* to your sense of God's absence, I need to warn you. You may at first think, as I often have, "Why was God present to all these others but not to me?" Nevertheless, such an examination of scripture—with the heartfelt desire to find God beside you—is bound to be rewarded. Perhaps you will realize, through others' experiences, that you've already witnessed God's presence in many miracles of with-us-ness but just never recognized them as such. Or perhaps reading for God's presence will prepare you to honor such miracles to come.

Reading the Bible in this way does not take faith. In fact, for those who don't already have faith in God, reading this hodgepodge of writings by ancient writers with the express purpose of finding evidence of God's presence is an important early step in the work of believing in God. Let's face it, some of those writings—like the genealogies and the wild apocalyptic visions of Daniel and Revelation—can be boring and difficult to follow and often, even after concerted reflection, not particularly enlightening. But think of that box of documents that you imagined receiving in the mail. Mere scraps of words that survived a life. Unarranged. Incomplete. Frustratingly unrelated to one another. Tedious and mundane. When you read them with the purpose of discovering the father you never knew, though, those documents become sources of important knowledge and thus interesting. Even receipts and scraps of news about forgotten people and events acquire meaning and relevance.

The simple existence of that box is also compelling. Someone collected all those documents and packed them up and sent them to you. At least *that* unknown person still exists, you consider as you go through the box's contents. *That* person saw a relationship between those documents and you. *That* person, in undertaking to collect and send the documents your way, must have cared enough about you to want you to know your heritage: the beaming father, his interests, his character, his story, his relevance to who you were and who you are now and who you will be in the future. As you read, the hazy unknown person these documents conjure becomes clearer, becomes the father you always longed for, a father who not only existed but who knew you and loved you and, in your consciousness at least, continues to exist. Reading to discover that father, in other words, develops in you a sort of faith in him. It also engages every wisp of the hope you had before you started reading.

Reading the Bible for evidence of God's presence is not, as I've said, how most believers read the Bible. Some read the Bible with the goal of finding nuggets of wisdom or applicable truth nestled among the accounts of wars and lineages and family horrors. Others read to confirm their faith. Some read out of vague interest or habit. Many believers read out of duty, seeking to fulfill a commandment they have unconsciously invented for themselves: Thou shalt read the Bible daily.

There is nothing wrong with reading the Bible with any of these purposes or even without a conscious purpose. But, as you have probably learned in some literature course in your past, the way you read determines, in large part, what you will find. If, in a period of loneliness for God's company, you read the Bible with the ardent and conscious goal of finding it, then you are likelier to be successful. And from the very first page, you will be in the heady company of fellow yearners who found and recognized God and delighted in God's presence.

1 ❧ Consider a distant relative you've always been curious about but who died before you were born or were old enough to know him or her. Perhaps this was someone famous in your family for certain actions or traits. First, write down everything you know about him or her. Now, give yourself the task of finding out more. Interview relatives who knew the person well. Look at family records and old photographs. Record what you learn about your relative that you didn't know before.

2 ❧ Do further genealogical research on your relative using tools available in libraries and on the Internet. The further you go in your research, the more diverse the records will become that reveal things about your relative. You may find birth, baptism, marriage, death, or burial documents; gravestones; news reports; historical information about a place and time; family records; land deeds; and any papers and objects that others may have saved—annotated cookbooks or a treasured collection of some sort—after the person died. You will likely discover that people outside of those you call your family have already undertaken research that intersects with your family's lineage. Such amateur genealogists often have information about your relative that your family has forgotten or never knew. You may find further genealogical information about your relative recorded by the Church of Jesus Christ of Latter-day Saints, which maintains extensive genealogical databases and library collections. Be as thorough and concrete in your own research as you can. Visit birth sites and graves, take pictures of yourself in these locations, jot down your feelings, do rubbings of gravestones. Keep records of everything you find and of all the sources you used to find it.

3 ❦ Write a brief narrative, as for younger family members, detailing everything you know about the relative.

4 ❦ How does this exercise change or complicate or deepen your sense of relation to the person? Are you or any other relatives like the person? How does it feel to claim this person as your kin?

CHAPTER SIX

Scriptural Evidence of God's Presence, Part 2:

A New Way to Read the Bible

SEEKING EVIDENCE of God's presence in the Bible requires a whole new way of reading. With that in mind, I want to explore what reading for God's presence might look like.

Let's take a passage that my husband read aloud to me one morning recently. Kris reads a chapter a day at the breakfast table. Having not been raised in the habit of daily Bible reading, I've never managed to stick with it much past Genesis, which I've read about a hundred times, since it's where I always start in my newest resolution. Soon after embarking, I get caught up in my other reading: magazines that arrive regularly and need to be read before the next one comes, books related to things I am writing about that I got through interlibrary loan and have to return soon, novels and other books people pass on to me as must-reads that accrue on my nightstand and eventually make it down to the breakfast table. When I look across the table at Kris with his Bible, I feel guilty, and often, to compensate, I substitute his Bible loyalty for my own by having him read aloud or retell the passage he's just read. We then discuss it, and our resulting devotional is my favorite—and often most meaningful—way of sharing God's company with someone else.

Kris, in any case, read aloud to me the beginning of Luke 6, in which Jesus was passing through some grain fields one Sabbath and his hungry disciples picked grain and ate it. Some Pharisees were also present.

"I wonder what *they* were doing in that field," Kris said, and we interrupted our reading to speculate. We couldn't agree on an answer, though, so Kris kept on reading.

The Pharisees asked Jesus why his disciples were "doing what is unlawful on the Sabbath" (Luke 6:2), by which they presumably meant "working" by gathering heads of grain and rubbing them in their hands to remove the chaff before eating them. In answer, Jesus reminded all present of a story from scripture in which David, in flight from Saul, entered "the house of God" and shared with his hungry companions some of the priests' consecrated bread, which, Jesus explained, "is lawful only for priests to eat" (Luke 6:4). Then Jesus declared that "the Son of Man"—a name he often used for himself in the gospels—was "Lord of the Sabbath" (Luke 6:5).

"Why do you suppose the disciples were doing that?" Kris asked me, after he read the story. I misunderstood his question as being about the probable inefficacy of the disciples' trying to satisfy their hunger with a few grain heads, a practical consideration that has always bothered me about the story. I mean, it doesn't seem to me that chewing on a few grains of wheat or barley or whatever it was would do much to assuage real hunger.

What Kris actually meant, though, was something else altogether: namely, why, indeed, as the Pharisees asked, were these devout Jewish boys doing something that everyone would have known was unlawful on the Sabbath? We posited that the disciples—mostly fishermen and ordinary workers—were perhaps uneducated in the finer points of their faith. Could it be that they actually *didn't know* that grain-rubbing was work and therefore unlawful on the Sabbath? Or does the passage present a sect dispute, in which the Pharisees were picky about things that didn't bother other Jews?

Kris and I compared the passage to the accounts of the same event in Matthew and Mark, noticing that each account makes clear that it was only the disciples, and not Jesus himself, who rubbed and ate the grain. We noticed, too, that directly following the grain-rubbing episode in all three gospels was another confrontation about Jesus himself illegally "working" on the Sabbath: While preaching in the synagogue, Jesus healed a man with a withered hand.

In the withered-hand story, the Pharisees had the same objection, unvoiced this time, and Jesus responded to their unspoken question with a question of his own: "I ask you, which is lawful on the Sabbath: to do good or to do evil, to save life or to destroy it?" (Luke 6:9). His answer made the Pharisees so mad, according to Luke, that afterward they plotted "what they might do to Jesus" (Luke 6:11). The other gospels are more explicit: The Pharisees plotted to kill Jesus.

Kris and I discussed the connections between the two episodes and the irony that Jesus' comparison of saving life versus destroying life on the Sabbath referenced both his own act of *saving* life through the healing and the Pharisees' secret intention to *destroy* life by murdering Jesus.

My husband's and my goal in reading the passage together was to expose ourselves to God's word and consider how it might pertain to our lives. Resting on the Sabbath is an elusive goal for us, and we talked about what the stories of picking and eating grain and healing the withered hand on the Sabbath might tell us about what our own Sabbath rest ought to look like. Reexamining the two stories now with the specific intention of seeking in them evidence of God's presence yields other information.

First off, in the grain-rubbing story, both the disciples and the Pharisees are in the presence of someone who claims divinity by referring to himself as "Lord of the Sabbath" (Luke 6:5). If Jesus' claim is true, in other words, then everyone mentioned in the account is in the presence of God, though they may not know it. Their collective experience of God's presence, here, is a confrontation in which the two groups involved—the disciples and the Pharisees—experience God in different ways.

For the disciples, God is, in this instance, their friend and companion. Until the confrontation occurs, the day is a Sabbath like any other. Jesus and the disciples have probably been to one synagogue and are on their way to another, as they often were, passing through the grain fields that would have surrounded most towns. Although the disciples are the hungry ones who've committed the "crime" with which the Pharisees confront Jesus, they remain silent in all three accounts, suggesting through their nonparticipation in the dispute that Jesus is not merely their companion but their spokesperson— their voice—and the one responsible for their actions. Jesus is, in other words, so fully "present" with the disciples in the moment of the confrontation that he seems to *be* them. Also, although Jesus apparently did not join the disciples in picking, rubbing, or eating the grain, he is, as their leader, answerable for their crimes and responsible for defending them. This passage demonstrates, in other words, that being in the presence of God can be an utterly passive experience in which one allows God to act and speak on one's behalf.

The Pharisees are also in God's presence, and we can vicariously experience God's presence in examining the confrontation from their perspective too. The God the Pharisees unwittingly encounter in the story of the grain rubbing is hardly a friend and companion or spokesperson but rather an adversary with considerable power and authority in their own area of expertise. Although it's the disciples whose behavior the Pharisees fault, they clearly know that neither the disciples nor their peccadilloes are what's at issue. The Pharisees engage only Jesus. And, in their next confrontation on the subject of proper Sabbath behavior, it is also Jesus alone—not the disciples in attendance—whom they will plot to kill. The Pharisees' experience of the deity in this episode is of a person who stands up to them, who quotes scripture in response to their attacks, who challenges their faith with audacious claims, and who counters their smug antagonistic questions with equally aggressive questions of his own.

"Have you never read what David did when he and his companions were hungry?" Jesus asks these scripture experts (Luke 6:3). Then, without giving them a chance to answer, he proceeds to remind them. Jesus, here, is the God of Job, demanding,

> "Will the one who contends with the Almighty
> correct him? . . .
> Prepare to defend yourself;
> I will question you,
> and you shall answer me." (Job 40:2, 7)

The Pharisees perceive the disciples' leader—who preaches in the synagogue and knows scripture as well as they do and blasphemes that he is the "Lord of the Sabbath"—as someone who ought to be following their rules. They're also aware that Jesus' views are so attractive that they'll need to get rid of him if they want to stay in power. In Jesus' presence, they feel anger and murderous hatred. The Pharisees experience God's presence, in other words, as a threat capable of undermining their own supremacy and therefore to be feared.

Interestingly, although sin is frequently thought of as going *out of* God's presence, the Pharisees commit the sin of premeditating murder while *in* Jesus' presence. Apparently, in other words, it is quite possible to sin while in the presence of God. Also, Jesus is aware of what the Pharisees are thinking and planning. He not only answers their unvoiced questions but challenges them with questions of his own. Whether they took his questions seriously we don't know, but if they did they were surely discomfited. Being in God's presence, in summary, can be an unsettling experience.

In answer to Kris's question about why the Pharisees were with Jesus and his disciples in that field in the first place, it occurs to me now that the Pharisees, like the disciples, probably *sought* Jesus' presence. They were surely curious about this fellow preacher, however much they may have disdained him. Possibly, without believing Jesus really was God, they were as hungry for God's presence in Jesus as were the crowds who surrounded Jesus wherever he went. Curiosity and secret hunger draw many into God's presence, I'm guessing. Certainly they drew me.

We may wonder where God the Father is in the linked stories of the grain rubbing and the withered hand. There are only a few episodes recounted in the gospels in which God spoke directly from heaven and was thus audibly present to those in attendance. Elsewhere in the gospels, Jesus invokes God's presence, as any other believer might, by addressing his Father in public and private prayers. In the grain field, though, God the Father figures in only indirectly. In one of the three gospel accounts of the incident, Jesus quotes a scriptural passage in which the Lord exhorts the Israelites, "I desire mercy, not sacrifice" (Matthew 12:7 and Hosea 6:6). And in all three accounts Jesus speaks of David and his companions entering "the house of God" looking for something to eat (Matthew 12:4, Mark 2:26, Luke 6:4). Jesus makes his Father real to his disciples and the

Pharisees—and to us, future readers of this passage of scripture—as a quoted voice and a presence in the temple.

Jesus' remarks about David in the house of God also invite us into the presence of God through that story. The account begins, "David went to Nob, to Ahimelek the priest. Ahimelek trembled when he met him, and asked, 'Why are you alone? Why is no one with you?'" (I Samuel 21:1). David, here, is hardly more than a boy, fleeing King Saul, who once loved him and now inexplicably hates him. Nevertheless, the high priest is so terrified that, when David demands bread, he offers the only bread available in his priestly household: "the bread of the Presence" (I Samuel 21:6)—that is, special bread that was offered daily in the temple in remembrance of God's provision and sustaining presence and that, when replaced with new bread, became the priests' primary sustenance. The bread of the Presence is thus, for priests, not merely symbolic of God's presence but, quite literally, their daily bread. In sharing this bread with David and his companions, Ahimelek shares God's presence.

Thus, when Jesus, in justifying the disciples' behavior, sends his Pharisee accusers as well as contemporary readers to the story of David and his companions eating the consecrated bread, he is suggesting that God is present to the Pharisees and to us in the same way as God was present to David and his companions. And present in the same way God was present to Ahimelek and the other priests when they offered up and later ate the bread of the Presence. And present in the same way that Jesus—who referred to himself as the bread of life—is "present" to believers to this day.

God is present and available to us in scripture; in our worship rituals; in the food we eat, which was God's first provision in response to human hunger; and in the person of Jesus, who was God's ultimate response to our deepest hunger for companionship with our Creator.

This one story, read for evidence of God's presence, models moments in daily life in which God might be in attendance. In camaraderie. In confrontation. In sin. God's presence might cause us to feel uneasy or even angry. Or our experience of God's company might be as natural to us as the disciples' companionship with Jesus. We might encounter God out in a field or in a church, among friends or with strangers, while relaxing and having fun or while fleeing our enemies. Our curiosity might draw us into God's presence, as might our hunger. Even simply eating and sharing food, which brings us into acknowledgment of God's ongoing provision, can invoke the palpable presence of our Creator and Provider.

God's presence, scripture reveals, can be experienced in a limitless variety of forms and in a limitless variety of venues. Examining others' experiences of God's presence in the Bible develops our capacity to imagine God in our own lives. If we expect to meet God at every moment, in every place, in every mood and circumstance, and in ways we haven't previously experienced, then we are likelier to recognize the presence of God when we encounter it.

─────────────

I ❧ Consider a biblical passage you already know to some degree—your favorite Bible passage, if you have one, or, if you don't, any story that you can remember. A story you were taught as a child. A story that has been in the news. A story someone else may have mentioned. *Without looking up the story or passage in a Bible*, write down as much as you can remember of it: the general plot, the characters, their motivations, any details you remember. If it is a story you especially like, record why. Now, *based entirely on your memory of the passage*, consider what hope of

God's presence, if any, the account seems to promise—to the characters involved, to the biblical writer, and to you.

2 ⚬∂ Now read the same story or passage in the Bible, specifically looking for evidence of God's presence. Read deeply. Consider each character in the story, how he or she perceives God, and any mention of God in the text. Is God actively present, mentioned, quoted, implied, absent? Study the context and read more than once, scribbling what you notice and any questions you have in the margins. If possible, read the passage in more than one translation; the Internet makes this easy. Become familiar enough with the passage to notice differences in wording and emphasis from one version to the next. If you have a study Bible, do *not* read the notes, which will introduce someone else's purposes and understandings of the text into your reading endeavor here. Use your hope for God's presence (not the cynicism that resists hope) as well as your best creative and reasoning skills—which you inherited from God, having been created in God's image—to consider what the story or passage might be saying about God's felt company in general. Record what you come up with.

3 ⚬∂ The book of Esther has always been problematic for theologians—famously for Martin Luther,[1] who wished the book wasn't in the Bible to begin with—because God appears to play little role in Esther's story. In fact, God is never once mentioned in the account of her life. Some speculate that God is omitted from the text because God actually *was* absent in the time of Esther, just as God's presence was scarce in the prophet

Samuel's boyhood, as recounted in I Samuel 3:1 ("The boy Samuel ministered before the LORD under Eli. In those days the word of the LORD was rare; there were not many visions"). Read Esther and consider the following questions. Is God actually absent for Esther and her cousin Mordecai? How does God's possible absence inform your understanding of Esther's and Mordecai's faith? Although God is not mentioned explicitly, is there any other evidence in the story of God's active presence? Compare what you believe about God's presence to the many references to people entering King Xerxes' presence in the story of Esther. Do you think Esther would enter God's presence as she enters her husband's? Why or why not?

4 ❧ If you are not a regular Bible reader, begin a regular Bible reading plan. Don't undertake too much—maybe once a week rather than every day—so that you do not fail too soon (as I so often have) and then give up altogether in frustration. Read sequentially, if you like, beginning with Genesis, or else follow some other plan. (The Internet offers many reading plans.) As you read, consciously look for evidence of God's presence—for the people involved in each passage you read, for the author of that part of the Bible, and, by extension, for yourself.

5 ❧ If you already read the Bible on a regular basis, devote a portion of your time to looking for evidence of God's presence —for the people involved in each passage you read, for the author of that part of the Bible, and, by extension, for yourself.

CHAPTER SEVEN

Coincidental Connections

$\mathcal{J}$UST A FEW YEARS AFTER I rediscovered God's presence, I started teaching English at the small Christian university where I still teach. I had, by then, gotten involved in a church for the first time in my adult life and was in the habit of reading the Bible frequently, if not regularly. I thought about matters of the spirit and my relationship with God all the time.

It was a happy, uncomplicated period of my spiritual development. Often, I woke up in the morning still puzzling through a passage of scripture I had happened onto the day before. Or with a line or two from one of the church songs from the previous Sunday rattling through my consciousness as I went about the business of morning. Most church music was new and thrilling to me in those days: both the traditional Protestant hymns, with their dense metaphorical language and gnarled theology, and the newer praise songs that repeated the same three giddy phrases over and over again. I hummed them in the shower and as I got dressed, careful not to get rowdy and risk waking my toddling daughters too early. At breakfast, I interrupted Kris's reading to get his take on the passage I'd woken up with.

As a lifelong Bible reader, he had already long since puzzled through the same passages I was struggling with and had tidy answers to most of my questions. I contemplated his conclusions and my own inevitable objections—*yes, but what about . . . ?*—as I cleaned up the breakfast dishes and got the girls up and ready.

Soon I was savoring one of my rare oases of alone time: the drives to and from work, during which I listened to the news on National Public Radio and groused about slow drivers and took note of the pretty pink sunrise or turkey buzzards circling overhead and the familiar reek of a dead cow somewhere. Invariably, by this time, something from the scriptural passage I had woken up with or the church song, or both, would seem to be at issue in everything else I noticed. It would crop up in one of the news stories. Or in an exchange of words I'd had with Kris or the girls that morning that I was still worrying about in the solitude of the drive. Sometimes, some element of the world outside the car confirmed, with startling clarity, what the biblical writer was saying. Often key words or concepts—from the radio, from my family, from the Bible, from the hymn—kept coming up, and I thought, *Wow, I've never really thought about that before, and now here it is again, and again. What a weird coincidence!*

At some point in the course of my drive—or perhaps later, after I had already arrived at school and the facilities man had made yet another comment relevant to my musings during our usual early morning chat—it would finally occur to me that maybe the recurring word or story or idea *wasn't* a coincidence. Maybe it was God sending me a message. Attracting my notice. Drawing me out of the hectic daily life of new motherhood and teaching classes and getting things done and into a world in which the God of creation might walk beside and converse with mere humans such as me.

And so, in my first free moment, I got out the study Bible I kept in a cupboard of my desk and looked at the passage again or used the Bible's concordance and cross-references to ferret out the scriptural underpinnings of the song I kept humming. I protested my way through the pat explanatory notes at the bottom of the page and scribbled in the margins comments I would later find indecipherable.

By midmorning, after I had taught a class and was back in my office for a while before teaching my next one, I was uncovering meanings in what I had been thinking about that had not previously occurred to me. Sometimes, by then, the puzzle of scripture had elucidated itself. And sometimes not. Sometimes the passage I had woken up with baffled me even more profoundly after all my meditation, and I thought, *This is not as one-dimensional as Kris or the songwriter or the commentators in my study Bible want to make it.*

Either way, the repeated words and images—which by now had emerged from my students' mouths as well—gradually coalesced into a compelling revelation. It was usually some simple notion, really, such as that God was a parent like me, or that Peter had experienced genuine faith, if only fleetingly, when he stepped out of that boat and felt the water solid beneath his bare foot. I could have learned the same truth from a commentary on the Bible or from a well-preached sermon. These revelations were more powerful, though—more convincing and relevant, more true—because they had insisted themselves upon my notice through the medium of my own experience and reflection.

All the while, in any case, I felt God standing by. Not concurring necessarily, it seemed to me. Not even wanting me to get to some specific right answer. Rather, merely laying a loving forearm across my shoulders and leaning in to consider the matter too. Enjoying my interest, my presence, the way a parent enjoys the rapt attention of the child watching a bug or listening to a bedtime story.

Later, at coffee with my colleagues, I made my announcement. "God was talking to me on the radio again," I told them.

They looked alarmed even before I got to what it was God had said to me. They didn't know what to make of the God I worshipped, who broke into *All Things Considered* on my car radio and spoke to me from the mouths of my daughters, the facilities man, my students.

Or rather, they didn't know what to make of *me*. I was apparently a Christian. I had signed the statement of faith our university requires of faculty. And I had the habit (also alarming to some of my colleagues) of bringing obscure lines of scripture into the most mundane collegial prattle about local real estate prices or whatever we were voting on at the next faculty meeting. But then, I was equally prone to making these wacky pronouncements about God—speaking to us directly, indeed!—as I was to rejecting out of hand the conventional Christian wisdom on most topics. *Perhaps she isn't a Christian at all*, I imagined them thinking, *but just some kooky New Ager*. And, as if in confirmation of their suspicions—having perhaps just dropped a passage from Jeremiah or Micah into their laps—I now mentioned, by way of support and concurrence, an article from *Saveur*, my favorite cooking magazine, or something one of my students had said in class that morning or perhaps those buzzards I had noticed on my way to school.

Here's the thing. God uses it all—every bit of it, all the time—to reach over to us and snag our attention. The Bible. The media. The created world. Family members and co-workers. Friends. Enemies. Strangers. Cattle. Pets. Our work. Our successes and failures. Our struggles—these last more than anything else, I think. Throughout the day, every day, our consciousness vibrates with opportunities to notice and enjoy God's presence.

Soon after embarking on any sort of scriptural study and the intentional plan to notice God in your life, you will likely become aware of similar connections and concurrences between the things of your life and what you are reading. If you are like me, your inclination will be to discredit such repetitions and confluences of ideas, if you pay any attention to them at all, as mere coincidences. These flukes of fate, I would argue, are actually crucial moments when God is nudging our notice. Luring us out of our own natural self-absorption. Drawing us.

Drawing is a word perhaps overused in the context of faith, but I can't resist its underlying argument: that God pursues *our* notice and company just as we pursue *God's*.

God says as much, again and again, begging us to turn back and seeming perplexed at our absence and perdition:

> I have not spoken in secret,
> from somewhere in a land of darkness;
> I have not said to Jacob's descendants,
> "Seek me in vain." (Isaiah 45:19)

Instead, God promises, as if willing us Godward, "You will seek me and find me when you seek me with all your heart. I will be found by you" (Jeremiah 29:13–14).

God's desire for human companionship and notice is characterized as bitter jealousy: "The LORD, whose name is Jealous, is a jealous God," God tells Moses (Exodus 34:14), and the first of the Ten Commandments addresses this jealousy:

> I am the LORD your God, who brought you out of
> Egypt, out of the land of slavery.
> You shall have no other gods before me.

> You shall not make for yourself an image in the form
> of anything in heaven above or on the earth beneath
> or in the waters below. You shall not bow down to
> them or worship them; for I, the LORD your God,
> am a jealous God. (Exodus 20:1–5)

A jealous God—like a jealous lover or a jealous child—longs for the unshared attention and attendance of the beloved. If we act on our own longing by seeking God, God invariably responds by seeking and drawing us in return.

Our natural inclination, regrettably, is to pull away from God. We are attracted elsewhere, in all directions, in any direction but God's. I picture, in saying this, not the prodigal son, stomping off, his inheritance in his pocket and hateful words still in his mouth. Not Cain or Judas. Rather, I see a small child on one of those tethers that parents sometimes use at the mall. The child doesn't really want to be gone from the parent on the other end of the tether so much as to get at what's just beyond reach—to grab it, look at it up close, taste it, feel its realness on the tongue.

I don't want to underrepresent, here, the repulsiveness of sin or our own culpability for our misdeeds. But, the sins I've witnessed—including my own, past and present—haven't usually seemed like conscious efforts to get away from God. Rather, they have been attempts to please the self: to explore what's beyond the immediate circumference of God's presence, to experience it, to know more. And pleasing oneself, I would argue, is not, in and of itself, sinful. Indeed, the impulse to please the self derives from who we are as creatures made in God's image. Like the Creator, who declared all of creation good and walked in the garden enjoying it, we, too, value good things: the created world, one another, knowledge. God wants us to enjoy creation. And Jesus sums up all of the Law and the Prophets into two great commandments: the first to love God and the second to love others *as ourselves* (Matthew 22:37–39). Not *instead of* ourselves, as the passage is often preached. We are expressly commanded to love not only God and others but ourselves.

Sin, when understood as the attempt to please the self, is not exactly a straining to get away from God, but what comes afterward, when—lacking that tether and wandering off from God unawares, or perhaps having pulled so hard that the tether broke—we get away from our parent entirely and become so absorbed in what drew us away, so caught up in it and perhaps injured by it and settled into its habits, that we lose track of where we are and how to get back to where we were. Everything looks different. We turn in every direction, yearning, searching in vain. *Where*, we ask, *did God go?*

Once, a student of mine wrote an essay about getting involved in a lifestyle she ended up regretting. She had just gotten her first job as a clerk in a bookstore at the mall, and one of her co-workers invited her back to his apartment to smoke dope. Having never used marijuana or any other drug before, she was curious, and the guy seemed pleasant enough, and kind of good looking, so she agreed. When she got to the guy's apartment, though, she had second thoughts. The apartment was dim, filthy, and littered with fast food containers. It smelled sickening.

She wanted to turn around and go home, she wrote, but she was "already there." She woke up the next day in the co-worker's unwashed bed and ended up struggling with addiction and creepy relationships for years afterward.

That, I think, is how sin typically works. Without consciously intending to go away from God—sometimes without even recognizing that we were ever *with* God in the first place—we suddenly find ourselves "already there": outside of God's presence. Or so it seems to us. We feel alone. We search in every direction, wondering where God went, or if God exists at all. And only later, having happened on a way back, do we realize that God was there all along, calling to us from the distance, gesturing, trying to get our attention.

Biblical writers typically characterize interactions with God as visions, dreams with clear messages, visits from angels, voices in the night. I have known people who have experienced God in such ways. One saw Jesus, dressed in jeans, standing at the foot of his hospital bed. Another observed an angel—which looked not at all like a person, he said, but like a massive gridwork of sorts—hovering around a house. Another dreamed of Satan, nightmare-real, and woke up knowing what course to take. I envy these experiences.

My own interactions with God—the very foundation of my faith—amount to little more than the recognition of God's hand in the arrangement of details in my daily life. When I am alert, I move through the day as a combination lock being opened, trembling slightly as each special number, out of all possible numbers on the dial, jolts into alignment. *Oh*, I think, as the lock falls open. *Oh!*

But it is not the thing learned—some biblical truth, enacted or emphasized through the minutiae of daily living—that I cherish so much as the constant reminder that God is in it all, every aspect of my life and the lives of those around me. Present. Involved. Even if I don't actually see God's face or hear God's voice, thundering or murmuring, or feel the weight of God's hand on my shoulder. The more attention I pay to God's potential presence—not only by expecting it everywhere but by crediting seeming coincidences as evidence of God's ongoing attendance—the more real that presence seems.

God is, as God told Moses and tells us, intensely jealous. Consider what it means to be the object of such jealousy. Like a lover, like a child, God craves our full attention, the most essential expression of love. God longs for our companionship and tries, continually, to claim it. Finding even a glint of similar interest on our part, God responds with delighted demonstrations of omnipresent attention: repeated words, concurrences of thought, sudden swellings of the perceived world into transparent displays of the world beyond our senses. In my experience, the more eagerly I pursue God and credit the resulting coincidences and revelations as valuable evidence of God's own pursuit of me, the more of such events I experience—and the more convinced I am of God's silent, invisible, intangible presence.

I ❧ One way to notice more of the coincidences of daily life is to record them. Writing down what you have experienced enables you not only to reexamine them but also to credit their accumulation as evidence of real and meaningful interaction with an otherwise unseen, unheard, untouchable God. As you follow the path of your longing into the presence of God— especially if you have already begun reading the Bible on occasion or attending a church service—keep a written record of your progress. If you already journal on a regular basis, this record might take the form of an addendum to what you already record about your life. Set it off from your usual entry by using a different color pen or enclosing it in a box. If you don't journal, or have tried to in the past and found it onerous, consider keeping a simple list—in a notebook dedicated to this purpose —of coincidences and revelations that occur to you.

Whatever format you use, give your record a title, such as *God in My Life* or *Evidence of God's Presence* or *Blessings*. (A title original to you is even better.) Titles help writers to be more intentional and focused about what they write. Date each entry and be sure to record any relevant scripture or other resources (such as the name of a radio program or book or magazine article) for future reference.

2 ❧ If you like to write, you may want to use parts of your list of coincidences and revelations to write personal essays about your experience for others to read. This is how I began writing about my own spiritual life. The resulting essays have become my most satisfying way of praying—that is, communicating with God. Such essays, of course, will be your own creation, so I will only make a few writerly suggestions here:

a ❧ Be as concrete as you can. Use objective language that actually describes—*pale yellow, curdled, banana-y*—in lieu of or in addition to subjective words like *beautiful* and *bad*. Use all your senses, not just sight.

b ❧ If you are telling a story or giving an anecdotal example, begin with some sort of an expression of time and cut out as much back story as you can.

c ❧ Read what you write aloud to someone else and then revise.

CHAPTER EIGHT

Memory

THE EARLY DAYS of my adult faith, as I have said, were happy and uncomplicated. Noticing God in those days took little effort. Indeed, it was difficult *not* to notice God's meddling in my life. I saw God everywhere. I spoke of God all the time. I bored and alarmed others with my preoccupation with matters of the spirit.

Soon, though, the business of living—which has its own jealous demands—resumed. I had two toddling daughters, a widowed mother-in-law living on our farm, a new teaching job at the local school followed by another new job at a nearby university, an additional part-time job helping my husband with big seasonal farm chores—haying, weaning, selling animals, calving assistance—and all the claims on my attention that attend such responsibilities. Soon, many activities I enjoyed before I became a wife/mother/teacher/ professor/farmer—that is, hanging out with current friends and corresponding with distant ones, writing stories, making art, reading —dwindled into wistful memories. I was just too busy.

Similarly, without intending to, I stopped noticing God's presence as much, stopped looking for it. I read the Bible less frequently and nodded off at church. Before I knew what had transpired, I found myself in another place, spiritually speaking. Not unbelief, exactly, or even the spiritual ennui that most believers suffer from on occasion. Not even complacency, really, since, whenever I took note of my new spiritual surroundings, I was not content.

Rather, I entered a place of spiritual oblivion. I simply stopped perceiving all the evidence of God's presence that I had come to cherish. Gradually, unintentionally, I began to live from one day to the next in just about the same way as I had lived before I became a believer, except that now I tacked a little prayer onto this or that worry. *Father God*, I prayed, *help me know what to do about Charlotte's thumb-sucking. Holy Spirit, please speak for me when Lisa and I have our talk about class scheduling. Oh, Jesus, let Kris not be so stressed all the time.* As soon as I had prayed my little prayer, I was done with God. Most times, I didn't even notice, or rejoice, when my prayer was answered. By then, another worry had already laid claim on my relationship with God, and the old one was forgotten.

I forgot not only yesterday's problems and prayers but the very core of my own faith history: the longing, the relentless seeking, the daily discoveries of God's involvement in my life that had made me a believer in the first place. Somehow, my faith, over time, shrank to empty habit, something I *should* be doing or feeling rather than the daily fulfillment of my desires and hopes.

It's difficult to explain how this could have happened. A friend of mine suffering from marriage difficulties once told me she couldn't remember why she had married her husband. She must have loved him, she said, but she couldn't recall a single detail of her early married life that would verify that she ever did. *Who was I when I met him?* she wonders now. *What did I want? What did I expect?* If she could just remember being in love, she told me, then she thought she could find a way to stay with him. It was like that with me and God. I still thought of us as together, somehow—I still called myself a believer and thought of God as my parent—but, in the busy-ness of living, I lost track of what that really meant.

Sometime during this period of oblivion, several years into my faith, I came across a journal I had briefly kept back when my faith was still new. A fellow teacher named Mitzi—younger than I was but a lifelong believer—had given me a blank book for Christmas. Its cover was a field of watercolor wildflowers—lavenders, pinks, greens —and Mitzi had labeled it "A Blessing Book" on the first page. Although I found the book was a bit cutesy, I nevertheless used it to keep a detailed account of three weeks of my life from that time. My disagreements with my husband. Our money troubles as farmers. Childrearing difficulties. Conflicts at work. My night worries. Eleven entries just like those in the diaries I had sporadically kept as a teenager, but with one big difference: I repeatedly compared the events of my days to what I was reading in the Bible. The entries were about as far from blessings as they could be. Rather, they recounted struggles, worries, discord—doggedly accompanied by strangely peppy-sounding efforts to see meaning in my grievances. Or, more exactly, to see the direct intervention of God in the everyday details of my life.

In one entry, I interpreted my boss's micromanagement of a program I administered as evidence of my *own* unwillingness to submit to authority, and I found hope in Peter's promise that "the God of all grace" would "restore" me and make me "strong, firm and steadfast" (I Peter 5:10). The word Peter used for *restore*, I noted—I've no idea where I found this out—was the same Greek word he would have used for mending the holes in a net. In another entry, I considered how best to confront a co-worker's misbehavior in light of Paul's counsel to "restore"—the same word Peter used!—fellow sinners "gently" (Galatians 6:1). Meanwhile, my husband and I were having one of those convoluted early marriage fights involving potty-training issues, his mom's constant involvement in our day-to-day routine, and whether or not to get out of farming entirely; and I blithely wrote, "I should be wanting to do God's will in this. I still too desperately want God's will to be the same as mine."

If there were no record of this admonition to myself, no record of those three weeks of living by faith, they would be gone forever. In the period of spiritual oblivion in which I found myself in the years that followed, I could not even recognize the earnest person who wrote those eleven entries. Time had transformed me into a person inexplicably unaware of my constant need for God and incapable of desiring God's will over my own. Incapable, even, of recognizing God's ongoing involvement in my life. Although more mature in every other way—older, wiser, and by then the conscientious moral coach of my own children and whole classes of befuddled students—I was a spiritual adolescent at best. I lived in the moment. My life was too hectic to admit much of a future beyond a scribbled to-do list, and I had not yet cultivated one of the primary skills necessary for distinguishing the presence of an unseen, unheard, untouchable God: remembering.

The Bible—especially the writings in the Old Testament, many of which employ mnemonic structures, such as repetition and anagrams of the Hebrew alphabet, to aid in memorization—is one emphatic charge to remember. The book of Deuteronomy, by way of example, catalogs dozens of explicit warnings against forgetting. "Only be careful," Moses commands the Israelites, "and watch yourselves closely so that you do not forget the things your eyes have seen or let them slip from your heart as long as you live" (4:9). "Remember that you were slaves in Egypt" (5:15) and "remember well what the LORD your God did to Pharaoh and to all Egypt. You saw with your own eyes the great trials, the signs and wonders, the mighty hand and outstretched arm, with which the LORD your God brought you out" (7:18–19). "Remember how the LORD your God led you all the way in the wilderness these forty years" (8:2). "[R]emember this and never forget" (9:7)!

In a lengthy song near the end of Deuteronomy—in other words, at the conclusion of the Bible's first five books, a collection of writings seen as an integral whole known among Christians as the Pentateuch and among Jews as the Torah—Moses, near death, summarizes God's relationship with the Israelites and entreats them,

> Remember the days of old;
> consider the generations long past.
> Ask your father and he will tell you,
> your elders, and they will explain to you.
> (Deuteronomy 32:7)

After he sings his song, Moses dies, having never entered the Promised Land. His song—and the Pentateuch itself—are our primary remembrance of those generations long past.

Even the most steadfast believers are prone to forgetting, Moses seems to have known. He predicted that, once the Israelites reached their Promised Land, they would become distracted, as I did, by the very richness of God's provision, forgetting its source:

> When the LORD your God brings you into the land he swore to your fathers, to Abraham, Isaac and Jacob, to give you—a land with large, flourishing cities you did not build, houses filled with all kinds of good things you did not provide, wells you did not dig, and vineyards and olive groves you did not

plant—then when you eat and are satisfied, be careful that you do not forget the LORD, who brought you out of Egypt, out of the land of slavery. (Deuteronomy 6:10–12)

The Israelites were likely to forget not only the source of their satisfaction and rescue from slavery, Moses foresaw, but everything he was about to teach them about how to continue living in prosperity and freedom. So, before Moses issued the words of the Law, he prescribed several key memory aids: "Talk about them when you sit at home and when you walk along the road, when you lie down and when you get up. Tie them as symbols on your hands and bind them on your foreheads. Write them on the doorframes of your houses and on your gates" (Deuteronomy 6:7–9). One of the best methods for remembering God, as Moses suggests, is to systematically recount what one already knows, record it, and display the record in such a way as to reencounter it repeatedly throughout one's day.

Over the centuries, the church has taken up Moses' tutelage in remembrance in countless ways. Amish women wear prayer hats and Orthodox believers wear prayer bracelets—akin to those symbols the Israelites were to wear on their foreheads and hands—as physical reminders to pray continually. Others wear religious jewelry—St. Christopher medals, crucifix pendants, purity rings—to prompt faith in times of trouble or temptation. For similar reasons, religious statues and other faith artifacts are often prominently displayed in private households and public buildings. Churches use countless sensory reminders of the important moments in the narrative of their faith: crucifixes, crèches, candles, images of praying hands or Jesus carrying someone in his arms, palm leaves, crowns of thorns, the Stations of the Cross, hymns, oral recitations, incense, bread, wine. Church bells traditionally ring on the quarter hour to remind believers to pray on a regular basis. Church services themselves are ritualized acts of remembrance, in which key events of faith—such as Jesus' birth, death, resurrection—are acted out and thus ritualistically revisited by all in attendance.

From early times to the present, religious instruction has typically involved memorization—that is, systematized remembering. Before the age of computers and smartphones and other information storage devices, having a good memory was viewed not merely as a clever talent or useful skill but a moral mandate. (As a person famous among her acquaintance for her weak memory, I find this mandate discouraging—another of the spiritual gifts in which I am so lacking!) Children were trained through memorization, and well-known believers were often lauded for their amazing feats of memory, such as the memorization of the entire Torah. "Memory verses" and other memorization projects are still promoted in many religious circles to this day. Indeed, the theologian Augustine, an early father of the established church, argues in his spiritual memoir that memory—which he presents as the ability to know things beyond what we perceive through the senses—is the source of *all* knowledge of God. Augustine speculates that humans must be born with the memory of God's presence. How, otherwise, he reasons, would we know to seek or yearn for God in the absence of any material evidence that God even exists? To know God, Augustine argues, is to go inside oneself and revisit one's previous experiences of God's presence.[1]

Becoming aware of God for the very first time, I would posit along with Augustine, involves memory. I have many memories from my years as a nonbeliever of God's clear participation in my life. Once, as a teenager, drunk after a party and disoriented in one of California's dense early morning fogs, I fell asleep on the freeway. I thought I had pulled over to the shoulder but awoke to find myself in the middle lane, with cars zigging madly around me. Somehow I wasn't killed. My parents' car wasn't even dented. Looking back on that miracle later as a reluctant atheist, having lost even the vague consciousness of God I'd had as a child, I nevertheless sensed retroactively that I had been protected. The God I'd lost track of and not yet rediscovered—the God who, in my thinking, didn't exist at all—I nevertheless recognized as the source of protection and survival. And to recognize—to *re-* (again) + *-cognize* (to know)—something is to be aware that one has encountered it before. To recognize God is, in other words, to remember.

However miserable our circumstances when we emerge from the uterus—and many infants are born into unimaginable misery— we are nonetheless born with at least enough knowledge of the experience of gestation to expect a continuation of the protection, nourishment, warmth, and comfort that our perfect union with a wholly present parent afforded. From birth, we mouth instinctively for nourishment and nestle confidently into whatever arms offer themselves. We are born expecting not only food and protection from the elements, but comfort and love: to be held, touched, even spoken to, however meaninglessly at first. Deprived of such manifestations of affection and care, infants don't thrive and may even die. Our congenital expectation of love, I would argue, is the source of our longing for God.

We seek God later in life because our battered bodies and spirits remember—if only dimly, in a past obscured by lesser consolations and perhaps considerable unpleasantness—what it was like to be fully encompassed by a dependable source of sustenance, protection, and love. In longing for God's presence, we unthinkingly long for something we all once had: a fetus's creaturely confidence that it will be taken care of. When we discover God for the first time—when, even as adults, we recognize God's presence in our lives—we are grasping at that remote memory of true happiness.

It is not surprising, then, that Moses—and other prophets after him—constantly urged us to remember. Faith, and faith growth, depend on memory. Thus the advice of the nameless Teacher who wrote Ecclesiastes to

> Remember your Creator
> in the days of your youth,
> before the days of trouble come
> and the years approach when you will say,
> "I find no pleasure in them."— (12:1)

Thus, too, the comforting promise in Proverbs that if parents but "Start children off in the way they should go," then "even when they are old they will not turn from it" (Proverbs 22:6). Memory will bring them back to God.

Biblical believers, in light of such promises, practiced believing through various acts of remembrance. They frequently constructed memorials and named them. Abraham built altars wherever he encountered God. When Jacob woke to find himself in the presence of God, he set the rock he had used as a pillow on end "as a pillar and poured oil on top of it. He called that place Bethel," which is Hebrew for House of God (Genesis 28:18–19). The prophet Samuel likewise set up a stone he named Ebenezer—or "Stone of Help"—at the site of a battle victory in order to remember that "Thus far the LORD has helped us" (1 Samuel 7:12). Often the memorial was an action rather than an object, as when the Israelites commemorated the crossing of the Jordan by dividing into two groups across a valley from one another and shouting out the curses and blessings of the Law (Deuteronomy 27–28).

God sometimes explicitly commanded that events be routinely commemorated in a certain way. After stopping the flow of the Jordan for the Israelites to cross with the ark into Jericho, God told Joshua to have men "take up twelve stones from the middle of the Jordan, from right where the priests are standing, and carry them over with you and put them down at the place where you stay tonight" (Joshua 4:3). When they had carried out this command, Joshua told them, "In the future, when your children ask you, 'What do these stones mean?' tell them that the flow of the Jordan was cut off before the ark of the covenant of the LORD. When it crossed the Jordan, the waters of the Jordan were cut off. These stones are to be a memorial to the people of Israel forever" (Joshua 4:6–7). God gave similar instructions regarding circumcision and the Passover meal, and later Jesus would offer his disciples bread and wine and tell them, "Do this in remembrance of me" (Luke 22:19).

God erected memorials, too, such as the various covenants. After the flood, God set the first rainbow in the sky and told Noah,

> Whenever I bring clouds over the earth and the rainbow appears in the clouds, I will remember my covenant between me and you and all living creatures of every kind. Never again will the waters become a flood to destroy all life. Whenever the rainbow appears in the clouds, I will see it and remember the everlasting covenant between God and all living creatures of every kind on the earth. (Genesis 9:13–16)

It is the Creator of Heaven and Earth, here, who takes measures to avoid forgetting, so it must be that memorializing key moments of one's faith is no mere stopgap against forgetfulness—surely our all-knowing God doesn't share my memory problems!—but a sacred act.

Certainly God commends our efforts to remember our faith history. Malachi documents a period when the Israelites had all but given up on the presence of God, who seemed to be blessing only the evildoers that surrounded them. *Where is God?* they worried. *When will we see God's justice prevail?* God commented scornfully about their faithlessness. But then, Malachi reports, "A scroll of remembrance was written in his presence concerning those who feared the LORD and honored his name." God called those who constructed this holy memorial "my treasured possession" and vowed to spare them from destruction (Malachi 3:16–17).

Memorials are almost always sensory in nature. A rainbow. A recitation. A heap of stones. The fragrant smoke of roasting meat or incense. A mouthful of bread or wine. Things we can see, hear, touch, smell, or taste that evoke events that can no longer be seen, heard, touched, smelled, or tasted. Those who originally witnessed the event die. Their descendents scatter. Without some sort of physical monument or record, even the most memorable of events—a flood that drowned all but a handful of the creatures on earth or a miraculous rescue from murderous pursuers or the enslavement of one people by another—is destined to be erased through subsequent generations' self-preoccupation and the sheer passage of time.

Memorials also work best when displayed prominently. A rainbow fills the sky. A large, upright rock stands out on the distant horizon. Most churches that commemorate Jesus' offering his disciples bread and wine at the Last Supper present the bread and wine at the front of the church in a showy manner and are likelier to use an ornate chalice—or a handmade ceramic goblet—than the plastic cup the pastor used for orange juice at breakfast that morning.

However permanent and however prominently displayed, though, a memorial only works as insurance against future feelings of abandonment by God if people keep track of the story behind it. A big rock on the horizon is, in other words, merely a big rock, if we don't remember who set it upright and why. There are some old graves on my family's farm, a small circle of tabular stones clearly chosen or shaped as grave markers, but otherwise unidentified. The names and stories of the people buried beneath this intended memorial are lost to anyone who does not already know to look for the stones in our pasture. All that this memorial can teach the rest of us is that a number of people either lived near or passed through our fields sometime long in the past. And that those people died, as all of us eventually will.

I didn't keep the blessings book Mitzi gave me in a prominent place in my house. It vanished, as most of my belongings do, in the ephemera of family living: in our little used study, buried under stacks of books and magazines, layered among some folders of papers that my daughters had scribbled on when they were little, forgotten. I forgot what I had learned about God and myself in those few passionate weeks of new faith. Like Peter after his first bold steps out onto the water to meet Jesus, I soon got so distracted by the waves of duties and activities of my life that I forgot how my faith had, from the start, buoyed me up, and I sank into a habit of forgetting. I forgot the promises that had originally nurtured my hopes and lured me into faith. I forgot my own prayers from day to day and didn't even notice when they were answered.

And so, years passed, after my rather dramatic midlife conversion from utter unbelief to faith, when I lived, once again, outside of God's presence, as far as I could tell. Though I believed in God, I didn't sense God near me.

When I rediscovered the green and pink and lavender journal much later and leafed through its pages to see what I had written there, I was shocked by how close God had been to me in those early days of my faith and how distant, by contrast, God had become in the intervening years. Like my friend whose marriage was failing, I longed to return to the closeness and realness of my early relationship. Reading the entries, I felt as though a different person had written them. Another woman, not I, had noticed those parallels between the scriptural passages I was reading and my daily doings. A different person had sensed God's nearness. Like my friend, I thought, *If only I could remember what it felt like to know God the way I once did, then I could feel that way again.*

Unlike my friend, though, I had a pathway for a return to a sense of divine companionship: the brief memorial, recorded in my own handwriting, of a time when I enjoyed God's presence and received daily, even hourly, reminders that God enjoyed my presence as well. The blessings book not only ratified the enduring existence of a faith worn thin by the commotion of living but modeled the presence-evoking activities that I would need to follow to find my way back into God's company.

---

1 ❧ Keep a "scroll of remembrance" (Malachi 3:16)—that is, a blessings book—in which you give thanks for the ways you notice you have been blessed. Your book may evolve, as mine did, into a journal of your struggles to live out your faith or to believe at all, and that's okay. Just be sure to review the pages every once in a while and see if any of your struggles have been resolved or prayers answered. If they have, record that, too, and give thanks. Thankfulness is a crucial way of remembering.

2 ❧ Design a memorial for your own doorway. For practicing Jews, this is a small container called a *mezuzah*, which contains

a rolled up slip of paper on which is written Deuteronomy 6:4: "Hear, O Israel: The LORD our God, the LORD is one." Your memorial, though, could take any form: a similar box containing a scroll, a small poster or plaque, an image, or simply words written on the doorjamb. The memorial might display a passage of scripture that you think is important to reflect upon each time you enter your house, or it might recount a brief encapsulation of a story from your own experience of God's presence. Take the time to make this memorial presentable for outsiders, so that, if someone asks you about it, you are not ashamed to have them examine it as you explain. You might use a calligraphy pen or gold leaf or some other craft material to make it pretty.

3 ❧ Prophets of the Bible often dressed in a way that visually memorialized some part of their message for themselves and others. Elijah and John the Baptist wore rough garments of hair and leather belts, for example, symbolizing repentance and mourning. As a victim of violent crime in my twenties, I suffer from post-traumatic stress disorder (PTSD), the symptoms of which are exacerbated when I hear stories of female victims of violence—war refugees, hostages, and victims of rape—in the news. Sometimes I am moved to pray for them, and, when I am, I like to wear a certain outfit—a diaphanous white skirt specked with black and a matching tunic—that for me evokes these women, although I can't say why. I rarely think of wearing the outfit when there is not something going on in the world that threatens to trigger my PTSD symptoms. If I wear the outfit in a time of relative peace, I sense a commonality with victimized women I know nothing about—certainly there are many—and am moved to prayer. Buy—or make or assemble from clothes you already have—a memorial outfit for the purpose of remembering a cause or event of spiritual importance to you.

4 ❧ Commemorate—through a special meal or celebration— an event not already in the church calendar but from your or your family's or friends' own spiritual history. Try to devise specific tastes or smells to evoke the event. My widowed mother-in-law commemorates her husband's death every year by eating the meal they had on their honeymoon: roast beef sandwiches. Although my daughters and I never met her husband, we all know what the meal means, and whenever I eat a roast beef sandwich—even if it's not at my mother-in-law's house—I reflect on her loss of her most valued companion.

5 ❧ Begin your own spiritual memoir, which is nothing more than a memorialization of your development as a believer. No rules to follow here. Just as every person's journey into or out of or alongside faith differs, so everyone—even a nonbeliever— has a faith story to tell. There are countless published spiritual memoirs to use as models. A few of my favorites are Augustine's *Confessions*, Leo Tolstoy's *Confession*, Hudson Taylor's *A Retrospect*, Kathleen Norris's *Dakota*, Anne Lamott's *Travelling Mercies*, and chef Nigel Slater's utterly secular spiritual memoir *Toast: The Story of a Boy's Hunger*.[2]

CHAPTER NINE

The Faith Stories of Others

EVERYONE, EVEN THE most devoted atheist, has a faith story: a story of seeking, evading, finding, losing, accepting, rejecting, loving, hating, sensing, not sensing, hoping for, and/or despairing of a connection with our invisible, inaudible, untouchable Creator. Even those incapable of telling their story or knowing they have one—those with mental handicaps, for example, or newborns—have nevertheless perceived God's creation and thus have experienced God or suffered a sense of God's absence in our world. They have been cherished—or not. They may have been held and nurtured, or they may have been abandoned or abused. Whatever the details of their experience of life, a story relevant to their perception of God resides within them, as much a part of who they are as the blood progressing through their bodies from their hearts to their organs and limbs and nerve endings and to the invisible electrons juggling their ideas and unconscious impulses in this or that area of their brains.

Some tell their story often and everywhere; others guard it from all but intimates. Some refuse to talk about matters of faith at all.

Whether a person tells the story or buries or denies it, it exists and informs that person's beliefs.

A faith story is a story in progress. Unlike a literary story, it lacks an ending—in this life at least. It's more like a story in the news in that respect: focusing on spectacular events going on right now, casting only the briefest glance at the past, and usually ignoring the future entirely. News isn't news until it happens, as the saying goes, and seekers often view their spiritual life in that way—as something that hasn't happened yet and thus doesn't exist. If they haven't yet gotten religion, they think, then they have no spiritual life at all. Or, if they lost the beliefs they once had, then they no longer have faith, end of story. But they live on, and their story of loss or abandonment or fear or longing continues.

Like all stories, literary or otherwise, faith stories feature key characters, numerous episodes, conflict, and rising and falling action. The protagonist of the story—that is, the believer or nonbeliever whose story it is—may live a faithless life until a certain defining event, or the person may grow steadily as a believer only to fall into unbelief later and perhaps rediscover faith in the last moments of life. Some people live lives of searching, others lives of scoffing. Some devote an entire lifetime to the attempt *not* to have any faith story at all. But that, too, is a faith story—a sad one, I feel, but still a story, and often a compelling one, when I can get a person to tell it to me.

God is a crucial character in every faith story, whether the protagonist knows it or not. In some faith stories, God is an active participant. In others, God lurks in the background or seems to hide. Sometimes, God abandons the protagonist—or so the protagonist believes—by failing to mete out justice or by seeming absent during a catastrophe. Not infrequently, God is the antagonist of the faith story in permitting or even seeming to cause the pain or trouble that the protagonist suffers or witnesses.

Naturally, God's intangibility plays a role in most faith stories. How could it not? Imagine reading a novel in which one of the characters is invisible. How would one tell that story without taking the character's immateriality somehow into account? Indeed, faith itself— and the faith story that shaped it—might be defined as what one does with the idea of God in view of God's imperceptibility. The faith stories of atheists typically start and end with what they offer as the most obvious proof of the nonexistence of God—namely, the absence of any physical evidence of God's existence. Believers, by contrast, tell stories in which they depend on other evidence than the physical—such as answered prayer or an inexplicable experience of deliverance—to develop trust and intimacy with God.

Faith, in other words, requires trust. There are many believers who undertake impressive works of trust in their lives and have that story to tell. An unbeliever's story, by comparison, is about distrust and uncertainty. I have known several people who were victims of the Holocaust and other atrocities, and, understandably, every one of them tells a version of that story of unbelief. When I am with them, their up-close knowledge of a world which God appears to have deserted moves me, and their legitimate outrage rattles the foundations of my own faith.

Often an unbeliever's uncertainty and distrust is masked by cynicism or boredom. The inability to perceive God in ordinary, earthly ways leads some to tell a braggart's tale that omits God entirely or actively seeks to erase all evidence of the divine. God weaves an invisible thread through each story regardless: invisibly accompanying each of us, offering soundless advice, patting our shoulders undetectably, watching us as we sleep.

One person's faith story may be influenced by the faith stories of others. Most believers can identify another person whose story of recovery or growth or loss or struggle significantly affected their own faith development. Scornful nonbelievers or former believers often recount stories of hypocrisy on the part of others who call themselves believers. They may have grown up thinking, for example, that having faith means doing or not doing some action. *True believers*, they think, *go to church every Sunday*. Or, *a person of faith doesn't use certain language or drink alcohol*. When skeptics see a professing believer not doing the required behavior or doing the forbidden one—and, worse, not seeming in the least bit ashamed—they may conclude that the person is a liar and not a believer at all. If this liar happens to be especially likeable or admirable, then the storyteller's own faith—whether he or she defines it as faith at that point—may erode further. In such situations, people may say they lost their faith or call themselves lapsed believers, but what has perhaps actually happened is that their faith began evolving at that point from the one they grew up with into one that deemphasizes behavior or that rejects the notion of a prescriptive or punishing or personal God. Faith, in other words, absorbs and reflects and often reacts to the faith of others we encounter in life.

Once, when I first became a professor, I asked a colleague in biblical studies how he could teach the course in evangelism his department offers every year. My colleague was a strict Calvinist who, as I understood his brand of faith then, believed that our salvation or damnation was entirely predestined and out of our control.

"What's the point of evangelizing others," I asked him, "if everyone's spiritual destiny is already determined from the get-go?"

His answer surprised me.

"Evangelism's not about salvation," he said. "It's about faith development."

He traced a rising line in the air with his hand.

"This is hell," he said, pointing to the low end of the imaginary line. "And that"—indicating the line's other end—"is heaven. On earth, nobody's in either place. Instead, each person is somewhere in between. Here. Or here. Or here." He pointed to places on the line. "In telling someone about God, you're not trying to get them from hell to heaven, but from the spot where they are on this continuum a little bit further along in the direction of heaven."

As a fairly new believer myself in those days, I had advanced hardly a centimeter from where I had started out on my colleague's imaginary line, so this was new information. But before I could really take it in, he rubbed his hand through the air to erase the line he had drawn and replaced it with a different line, this one jagged and gnarled with ups and downs and loops and zigzags.

"And this is what a real person's progress toward—and away from—heaven probably looks like," he told me. "You may go steadily up," he said, gesturing, "and then straight down, back to the place where you started and maybe past it. You may stay in one place for a long time. Or you may hop up and down for years. Or you may circle around like this." His hands slashed and reeled through the air. "In evangelizing, a believer comes alongside another person wherever they are on that line and tries to help them up a bit. That's all it is."

My colleague's lines have stayed with me all these years. The first line he drew: steady and rising, the way I pretty much thought in those days that faith was supposed to go, even though it hadn't in my own spiritual history. And the second line, which scared me a little. I certainly recognized in that line's jagged rises and falls and spirals my own journey up to that point. Until that conversation, though, I thought that my journey had ended. I had reached heaven, and I was planning to stay there.

Could it really be that I might slither back down into my previous unbelief and corkscrew around awhile before getting back where I wanted to be when I died? I fretted. It hardly seemed likely. I was as certain of my faith in those days as I had been uncertain of it in the years that preceded it. Nevertheless, when I reflected on the stories of the faith heroes I was becoming acquainted with in the Bible, I knew that my colleague's grim depiction of the typical person's spiritual development was likely accurate.

Consider David, whose story is recorded in several books of the Bible. Consider the inspiring faith he displayed when, as a young boy, he challenged a seasoned soldier—a giant, in heavy armor, who had terrorized people for years—with his little bean flip. (My husband always points out to me that a bean flip and a sling shot are two different weapons—the one a Y-shaped stick with something elastic between the prongs and the other the pocket on straps that David slung through the air—but in the story they amount to the same thing: a toy used against an armed soldier.) Imagine David a few years later, fleeing the murderous rage and crazed jealousy of his king and one time employer. Upon finding King Saul asleep in a dark cave, David opts not to kill him. He's obviously on the rise, there, spiritually speaking. Now see David as a king himself, much more successful than Saul ever was in every way. David enjoys wealth, victory over his enemies, many wives and sons and daughters, and an enviable certainty that God loves him.

Look up! There's David on his rooftop, surveying his dominion —and ogling the married neighbor woman bathing in her garden below. (They didn't have indoor plumbing in those days.) After years of inspirational righteousness, David not only lusts after Bathsheba, but sends his servants to fetch her to his bed. And when she becomes pregnant, he arranges for her soldier husband to be killed in battle.

He later repents, of course, and writes lots of contrite songs about his faith, but he also looks away when one of his sons, Amnon, rapes Tamar, a daughter of David by a different mother. After an impressive beginning as a young man of faith, in other words, David becomes first a Peeping Tom, then a rapist and adulterer, then a murderer, and, finally, a pretty irresponsible father, the way I see it. Hardly the defender of the defenseless that one would like to see in a model believer.

At the end of David's life, when he was so old and feeble that his servants had to get a beautiful young virgin to keep him warm in the night, we're told that the king "had no sexual relations with her" (I Kings 1:4). Whether he spared the beautiful Shunnamite Abishag out of the impotence of old age or because of a kindliness he had by then acquired toward the powerless women surrounding him, he circled back on himself, story-wise. He could have sinned there, certainly, but he didn't, which represents another spiritual rise, in my way of thinking. In David's history, as in my own, I recognize the same notched progress of faith, the same loops and rises and steep falls that my colleague drew in the air.

And David's not alone. Consider the fisherman Peter, one of Jesus' best friends and most ardent disciples. When Jesus first called him, he dropped his nets and came, and his faith was so great he was able to walk on water—for a moment at least, until he saw the waves and sank. Later, Jesus asked his disciples, "Who do you say I am?" and Peter alone offered the right answer: "You are the Messiah, the Son of the living God" (Matthew 16:15–16).

Peter's crazy love for Jesus may be summed up in his response when Jesus wanted to wash his feet. First he balked in humility. But, when Jesus said that belonging to him required it, Peter cried out, "Then, Lord . . . not just my feet but my hands and my head as well!"

(John 13:9). Peter's faith and dedication were utterly convincing and spontaneous, if also wrongheaded at times, as when he lashed out with his sword and lopped off the ear of one of the high priest's servants—a man named Malchus, according to John 18:10—who had come to arrest Jesus. Jesus rebuked Peter, who watched, surely ashamed of himself, as Jesus touched the servant's ear and healed it. A few hours later, though, seized with dread that he might come to the same fate as his master, Peter told those who asked who he was that he didn't even know Jesus. Not just once, but three times in a row. This is the jagged, circling ascent heavenward of the man whom Jesus called the rock on which he would build his church (Matthew 16:18).

Follow the path of any believer lauded in the Bible. Every one of them has moments of great faith and moments of doubt. Abraham and Sarah. Isaac and Rebekah. Jacob. John the Baptist. Nicodemus. Consider "the prostitute Rahab" and the daughter-murdering warrior Jephthah: Both are ranked with Moses and the prophets by the writer of Hebrews (11:31–32). Consider the nameless woman with five husbands whom Jesus had a conversation with one hot afternoon at a well in Samaria (John 4). Consider Jesus' own mother, who witnessed evidence of her son's deity firsthand, but later thought he was insane and went with his brothers to fetch him home so she could protect him (Mark 3:20–35).

Consider the servant Malchus, who fell victim to Peter's sword. We know nothing about this man but his name and the episode of the ear and that he worked for the high priest, as he is never again mentioned in the Bible. Try, nevertheless, to imagine who he was before he met Jesus and who he became afterward and the accounts of his experience he might have offered to those around him. What would that man's faith story have been in the moment when, having reached Gethsemane to take custody of his boss's enemy, one of the enemy's ruffian followers chopped off his ear? Would it have been the same story a moment later, when the man being arrested touched him and put the ear right again? And what about later—after the arrested man was killed and some were saying that he had come back to life? Did Malchus hear about it and, remembering his own miracle, come to believe? Could that be why John went out of his way to include the servant's name in his gospel: so as to identify him for peers who had heard of him, an evil and despised man miraculously transformed through his experience of God?

Or was Malchus, as Martin Luther argued in one of his sermons,[1] also the unnamed official who, a few lines later in John's account of Jesus' arrest and interrogation, slapped Jesus in the face and demanded, "Is this the way you answer the high priest?" (John 18:22). Something about the circularity of Luther's reading is compelling: Jesus' hand touches Malchus' head to heal him, and Malchus responds by putting his own hand to Jesus' head to hurt him. Was Malchus famous among John's audience—and thus identified by name—as a particularly malevolent enemy of Jesus, who tortured and sought to demean someone who had healed him moments before?

We'll never know. But we are surrounded by people with similar, if not always so dramatic, faith stories. People who were just going along through life—doing their jobs, not thinking deeply about God—and suddenly became victims of violence. People who miraculously survived horrific injuries or diseases. People who thought one way and underwent a total transformation to the opposite way of thinking. People who turned on those who loved them or seemed untouched by the most obvious evidence of God's nurture and protection and restorative power. People whose faith nursed them through loss.

Once I sat in a lecture hall with a group of public school

seventh-graders while a survivor of the Apollo 13 disaster told that amazing story. My students sat rapt as the astronaut recounted the hopelessness of their plight—the spacecraft crippled by an explosion and pitifully off course—and how they confronted the terrifying knowledge that they would be unable to return to Earth and would, thus, soon, die. In the end, they converted the lunar module they were carrying into a lifeboat, got themselves back on course, and survived. Entirely through human ingenuity, the astronaut stressed, again and again. My students were aghast that the man didn't seem to think God had anything to do with his story, which to them, ingenuity notwithstanding, was clearly an example of divine intervention.

Whatever a person's story, it has the power to influence yours. It may confirm what you already think about God—or religion or other believers. It may cause you to question or even reject what you have so far believed. Even someone's story of faithlessness has the power to corrode or grow aspects of another's faith. The astronaut's story collided with what my students so far believed in their twelve years of life, and the impact of that collision became a significant component of their own faith stories—and of mine.

The faith stories of those around you—of not only your friends, relatives, and co-workers, but public figures like that astronaut and even strangers—have important power to help you see and hear and feel God's presence. Like the writings in the Bible, the faith stories of others bear witness to God's presence—or apparent absence—in the tellers' lives. And, like the stories of even the most exalted of biblical believers, the stories of others in your life will invariably have high and low moments. Unlike scriptural faith stories, though, the faith stories of the people around you were not carefully recorded and studied for thousands of years. Rather, the faith stories of others are rough drafts and, as I have said, still in progress.

Whether you want to or not, you are likely to be affected by many such stories in the course of a lifetime, and your story will likely figure in the stories of others. With that in mind, it is wise to consider how one might go about listening to others' stories in such a way as to nurture a sense of God's presence in one's own life.

One model for how to use others' stories in the pursuit of God's presence is the Queen of Sheba. Having "heard about the fame of Solomon and his relationship to the Lord" (I Kings 10:1), she traveled by camel from faraway southern Arabia to hear Solomon's story for herself. Jesus himself would later commend the Queen of Sheba for this endeavor: "The Queen of the South will rise at the judgment with the people of this generation and condemn them, for she came from the ends of the earth to listen to Solomon's wisdom" (Luke 11:31). The Queen of Sheba's faith story, as recounted in scripture, is brief, so I offer it here in its entirety, leaving out only a minimally related portion describing Solomon's riches:

> When the queen of Sheba heard about the fame of Solomon and his relationship to the LORD, she came to test Solomon with hard questions. Arriving at Jerusalem with a very great caravan—with camels carrying spices, large quantities of gold, and precious stones—she came to Solomon and talked with him about all that she had on her mind. Solomon answered all her questions; nothing was too hard for the king to explain to her. When the queen of Sheba saw all the wisdom of Solomon and the palace he had built, the food on his table, the seating of his officials, the attending servants in their robes, his cupbearers, and the burnt offerings he made at the temple of the LORD, she was overwhelmed.
>
> She said to the king, "The report I heard in my own country about your achievements and your wisdom is true.

But I did not believe these things until I came and saw with my own eyes. Indeed, not even half was told me; in wisdom and wealth you have far exceeded the report I heard. How happy your people must be! How happy your officials, who continually stand before you and hear your wisdom! Praise be to the LORD your God, who has delighted in you and placed you on the throne of Israel. Because of the LORD's eternal love for Israel, he has made you king to maintain justice and righteousness."

And she gave the king 120 talents of gold, large quantities of spices, and precious stones. Never again were so many spices brought in as those the queen of Sheba gave to King Solomon.

. . . .

King Solomon gave the queen of Sheba all she desired and asked for, besides what he had given her out of his royal bounty. Then she left and returned with her retinue to her own country. (I Kings 10:I–I0, I3)

Although the Queen of Sheba traveled a great distance and spent a lot of money to hear Solomon's faith story, she received it with a good deal more skepticism than one might expect, especially in view of Jesus' later praise of her willingness to listen to Solomon. She didn't just accept what Solomon told her outright, but instead first tested him "with hard questions" and "talked with him about all that she had on her mind."

Unlike the translation that I have used throughout this book—Today's International Version (TNIV)—most other translations say that the Queen of Sheba discussed with Solomon what was "in her heart," not "on her mind." (Also, the key Hebrew word in the phrase ל ב ב [lēbāb] is widely used elsewhere in the Old Testament and almost always translated as *heart*, even in the TNIV.) Saying that the Queen of Sheba had something "on her mind," in any case, doesn't really capture what's going on here. The Queen of Sheba was not merely interested in Solomon's ideas. Rather, she was struggling with a matter of the heart. She was, in other words, troubled. Solomon had something that I suspect she felt she didn't: not merely fame and riches such as she already enjoyed, not merely wisdom and success, but that "relationship to the LORD" she came to hear about. It was Solomon's faith story that "overwhelmed" her.

Again, saying that the Queen of Sheba was *overwhelmed* by Solomon's assets—his wisdom and wealth and his subjects' fealty and happiness—doesn't quite get at the intensity of her reaction. Other versions of scripture translate more literally that there was no more spirit—or *breath*, which is the same word in Hebrew—in her. The Queen of Sheba's response to Solomon's story was more than mere amazement, I'm thinking. Rather, it took her breath away: She lost, in that moment, something that had previously animated her. Her spirit. The very breath that gave her life. One might argue that she lost her sense of security in her own relative prosperity and power, perhaps, but I think it was more. The Queen of Sheba witnessed, in listening to Solomon, something very relevant to her heart and her spirit. Something involving being not only wise, but "happy," as she imagined Solomon's people must be. Something involving being not merely wealthy and successful and famous, but "righteous" and "just." God, she realized during her visit, *delighted* in Solomon and *loved* Israel. *Clearly*, she must have thought, *these people live in the presence of God.*

In seeking out Solomon's story, the Queen of Sheba had a sensory experience of the presence of God. She listened carefully to what Solomon had to say and examined the evidence of God's presence in Solomon's court with her own eyes. She smelled the fragrance of the burnt offerings, tasted the lush food God had provided these strangers, and raised a jewel-encrusted cup of wine to her lips. Witnessing all of this, she imagined Solomon's people standing before him, hearing his words as she did, and she guessed that they were, in consequence, "continually" happy. During the Queen of Sheba's visit, her life's yearning—to have her own relationship with her imperceptible Creator—was fulfilled. Thus it was that "King Solomon gave the queen of Sheba all she desired and asked for"— what she longed for in her heart and in her spirit—"*besides* what he had given her out of his royal bounty" [my italics]. She came looking for, and found, a real experience of the presence of God.

The Queen of Sheba's method of seeking God's presence is simple: Seek out other believers' stories, listen to them carefully, and test them with hard questions. Before you undertake to follow the Queen's example, though, let me offer some practical advice from my own years as a rather wistful atheist who also traveled the world in search, however unwittingly, of a relationship with God.

First off, when you ask people questions about their faith, many— perhaps most—will think that you are attacking them and will behave accordingly. If this happens, they will not only withhold the story you want to hear, but they are likely to say things that may undermine your own search for God by confirming whatever negative views of faith that you may already have. Avoid any sort of combative response to what the person tells you and make clear that you regard the person's story as a precious resource. Remember the Queen of Sheba's gifts to Solomon. Remember, too, how she made herself vulnerable by revealing all that was in her heart. Introduce the topic of faith by revealing your own heart's desire to sense God's presence, and try, in whatever way you can, to make your interviewees aware that you are not seeking to judge or debate their faith experiences but to learn from them.

There are also people, on the other hand, whose lifelong desire is for some yearning soul to come along and ask them about their faith. These are likely to behave as our dogs always do whenever a newcomer —especially one with small children—shows up at our house. That is, they will pounce on you in their excitement: inviting you to Bible studies and religious events and all sorts of churchy activities that may, once again, have the effect of impeding your search for God's presence by confirming whatever negative views you already have about certain beliefs, believers, religious activities, and so on. Proceed with caution.

Also, try to elicit people's *stories*, not the tenets of their faith. Focus not on what, precisely, a person believes—which is likely to be very different, at least in some crucial details, from what you believe— but on how the person came to believe it. Ask people what situations in their lives made them most conscious of God's presence and, most important perhaps, whether there had ever been times when they felt God was absent. People are likelier to tell you something you haven't heard before—something, that is, that might reach you when nothing else has—when they tell their own stories.

Finally, people believe all sorts of weird things. Test whatever they say with hard questions. Luke commends the believers in the church in Berea for approaching even the instruction of such esteemed teachers as Paul with as much skepticism as enthusiasm: "Now the Berean Jews were of more noble character than those in Thessalonica, for they received the message with great eagerness and examined the Scriptures every day to see if what Paul said was true" (Acts 17:11). The apostle John similarly cautions, "Dear friends, do not believe every spirit, but test the spirits to see whether they are from God, because many false prophets have gone out into the world" (I John 4:1). Be wary.

Consider people's faith stories in the context of their actions, first of all. People fail to live up to their own convictions all the time, of course, so don't expect a perfect alignment of beliefs and behavior in the people whose stories you hear. But do look for evidence that the person at least tries to live in accordance with his or her experience of God—that is, look for shame, in the instance of failure, and for a governing sense that the person acknowledges God's superior power and authority.

Most important, test people's faith stories, as the Bereans did, against the time-tested accounts recorded in scripture. Do this by looking up key words in your Bible's index—or concordance, as it's commonly called—and then reading at the places where that word is mentioned. Resist the urge to just find a verse that supports what a person tells you and then quit reading. As anyone who reads the Bible will tell you, you can find evidence in it to support just about any idea, and the same is true of many other books. Testing what someone preaches against scripture is not a matter of finding a sentence or two from the Bible to support it. Biblical scholars call pulling a line of scripture out of context in this way to substantiate a belief "proof-texting," and they advise against it.

Instead, read comprehensively—whole stories from the Bible rather than isolated passages. And dare to ask of the text the same sorts of hard questions that the Queen of Sheba asked of Solomon, a man who was so famously wise he was known to distant strangers and whose writings eventually became part of scripture. Jesus himself praises those who struggle with the stories of others in this way. Seek in scripture not merely proof that what someone says is correct, but a solution to your own uncertainty and cynicism. And remember, you are looking not for ideas but for genuine evidence of the presence of God.

1 ❧ Review in your mind others whose faith influenced your own. Consider especially those whom you admired and whom you knew to be believers as you were growing up—parents, grandparents, teachers, friends, and so on. What events in their lives caused them to sense God's presence or absence? If they are still alive and accessible to you, question them about their experience of the presence of God.

2 ❧ Systematically collect the faith stories of several believers around you now, using the method laid out in this chapter. Remember to focus your inquiry on your subject's life experiences, not on a defense of their beliefs that they may want to offer. Reread my warnings at the end of the chapter before you do, as even your closest friends may surprise you in their responses.

3 ❧ Seek out the stories of several people whom you suspect or know to be nonbelievers. Again, review the warnings at the end of this chapter beforehand and plan out questions that will elicit stories and experiences, not merely a defense of atheism.

4 ❧ Think back on an atheist of your acquaintance or someone whose behavior or attitudes toward faith or God challenged or negatively affected your own faith. Depending on how much information you have about that person's life experiences, try to "read" or imagine his or her story as I imagined that of Malchus, the servant whose ear Peter cut off and Jesus restored. What might have caused the person to have developed the

attitudes he or she had toward God? If you are still in contact with the person and on good enough terms to talk about sensitive subjects, probe gently to see if you might be able to find out a bit more of the person's faith story. If you feel secure in your own faith, consider ways you might walk alongside that person in his or her spiritual journey.

CHAPTER TEN

Indirect Messages from God

WHENEVER I READ the phrase, "The Lord said to me" in the Bible, I envy whoever it was that God interacted with so straightforwardly. I envy Abraham. Moses. Paul. I envy poor Hagar, the servant Abraham impregnated and his wife Sarah abused, who was pursued by God in the desert and exclaimed, "I have now seen the One who sees me" (Genesis 16:13). I envy even the murderer Cain, with whom God reasoned, as a parent might reason with a surly teenage son, "Why are you angry? Why is your face downcast? If you do what is right, will you not be accepted? But if you do not do what is right, sin is crouching at your door; it desires to have you, but you must rule over it" (Genesis 4:6–7).

Why doesn't God talk to me like that? I have often wondered. *No wonder biblical believers had such unfaltering faith*, I think, momentarily forgetting the episodes in their stories in which it's clear they *did* falter, just as I do. *No wonder they believed so effortlessly. God appeared to them, spoke to them. God told them precisely what they were to do and promised them very specific—and verifiable—rewards for doing it. How could they* not *believe?*

Thinking about others' experiences of God's presence, I wish myself into a world like the one I read about in Scripture, a world in which God and humans relate face to face. I would discuss my problems with God, just as Moses and Abraham did. Like them, I would probably also argue with God on occasion, just as I do with my family members and friends. No doubt I would enrage God with my ridiculous views and complaints, and God would surely put me in my place. But it would be worth it to have God, in person, correct me or persuade me or nudge me forward into righteousness.

Once, one of my students handed in a paper that changed my way of wishing, though. I can't remember what she had written about, but she referred, in passing, to God's "metaphorical" hands and face and body mentioned in scripture, and I couldn't figure out what she meant.

"How are these metaphors?" I asked in the margin, and she wrote me a long e-mail in response. References to God's body parts must be metaphorical, she said, because God *has* no body. "God is a Spirit, and has not a body, like men," she concluded, quoting, she said, a passage from the official creed of her denomination that she had memorized as a child.[1]

"But weren't humans made in the image of God?" I argued the next time we met. "I mean, wouldn't that mean that our bodies are just like God's?"

She explained—patiently, because I make no secret of my inexperience in matters spiritual to the veteran believers who make up the majority of my students—that the "image" of God was also figurative language. God's "image" didn't refer to what God *looked* like, but to God's divine traits and habits. Creativity, for example, and that God works and rests and values companionship and so on.

I took what I saw as her odd views to the faculty coffee hour later that morning for discussion with my more theologically experienced colleagues and discovered that I was in a minority of one among them, when it came to thinking that God had a body.

"What about God walking in the garden in the cool of the day?" I persisted. It had always been a favorite passage of mine, one in which the invisible, inaudible, intangible God I worship sounds refreshingly real. "And what about God putting Moses in the crevice of a rock and letting him see his backside?"

I was a literalist, my colleagues told me. Also heretical. Apparently a number of famous heresies over the centuries were based on the corporeality of God. My colleagues explained all this nicely, mind you, and even made apologies for using the word *heretical*—"*Unorthodox* would have been a better way of saying it," one of them apologized— but the exchange was nonetheless unsettling. So much for my fantasy of one day strolling through my own vegetable garden some cool evening with God by my side, helping me figure out how to rescue my tomatoes from *Fusarium* wilt.

"Think about it," one of my colleagues continued, pausing first to suck up some coffee through the little hole in the plastic lid of his travel mug. "How could God be omnipresent and also have a body?" We all thought about that.

"Maybe God's *not* omnipresent," I put forward. My colleagues looked at me as though I were suggesting that God was not good or powerful or holy.

"I mean, whoever said God was omnipresent in the first place? Don't the stories of Job and the tower of Babel talk about God being somewhere else than here? Looking down on us? Coming down to see what people were doing? How can God be somewhere else and everywhere at the same time?"

Metaphors all, I heard them thinking.

By then our coffee break was over, and I was left to rethink my unorthodoxy on my own. (Or to *repent* it—if, as a chapel speaker had recently argued, the etymological root of *repent* is to *rethink*.) Given my combative instinct when it comes to learning new things, though—and also my colleagues' collective inability to defend God's omnipresence very convincingly from scripture—I became even more determined to find myself to be in the right in this matter. I scoured scripture in the weeks that followed, collecting masses of evidence to support my view.

I also found a few scriptural passages supporting the view that God is omnipresent—such as when, through the prophet Jeremiah, God says so:

> "Am I only a God nearby,"
> declares the LORD,
> "and not a God far away?
> Who can hide in secret places
> so that I cannot see them?"
> declares the LORD.
> "Do not I fill heaven and earth?"
> (Jeremiah 23:23–24)

Most of what I read, however—references not only to God's face, hands, mouth, fingers, backside, and other body parts but also to an apparently audible voice—confirmed my initial belief in some sort of bodily existence of at least this "God nearby," if not the far off God who sees everything. I haven't figured out a way to reconcile God's omnipresence with the divine bodily elements so often mentioned in the Bible, but then, I also haven't figured out a way to reconcile Jesus' divinity with his humanness. Much, in faith, boils down to mystery.

In any case, my study of the corporeality of God took me somewhere I didn't expect to end up: I noticed that God interacts with people indirectly a lot of the time. Most of the time, in fact. More often than not, those fortunate enough to see or hear from God in scripture actually do so in a dream or a vision. In some biblical accounts, God alerts people through signs, such as the burning bush that Moses comes upon. And in other stories, angels and even plain old humans and, once, a donkey deliver God's message. The biblical figures who interact with God directly are in the extreme minority, and even these blessed ones are apparently lucky to survive the encounter. After promising to "come down on Mount Sinai in the sight of all the people" God repeatedly warns Moses not to let the people get close enough to actually "see" him, lest they be destroyed (Exodus 19:11, 21). And after Jacob spends the night wrestling with someone who turns out to be God, Jacob marvels, "I saw God face to face, and yet my life was spared" (Genesis 32:30). God surely observes us from heaven and may even descend on occasion to take care of some matter personally, but scriptural accounts of such direct divine interaction are dramatic, rare, and evidently dangerous. In the main, God communicates with humans in less direct ways.

Interestingly, even those scriptural heroes I initially thought of as being particularly fortunate in the area of direct interaction with God—the ones I envied—mostly heard from God indirectly. Paul, for example, to whom Jesus spoke directly, in the presence of others, fifty years or so after his crucifixion and resurrection. A flash of light blinded Paul and a voice from heaven told him, "I am Jesus, whom you are persecuting . . . . Now get up and go into the city, and you will be told what you must do" (Acts 9:6). After such a beginning, it seems reasonable to expect that Jesus would continue to interact with Paul in the same direct manner, but Paul's subsequent interactions—even the ones that immediately followed up on the voice's instructions—were all indirect. First, he had a vision of a disciple named Ananias coming to him and laying his hands on him. Then Ananias had a vision in which God informed him of Paul's vision and directed him to go lay hands on Paul. Paul's final communication from God in this instance arrived via Ananias himself, who dutifully carried out God's will (although not without arguing with God first—presumably during his vision—that Paul was hardly a worthy choice). So, after the initial burst of light and heavenly voice to get Paul's attention, God used two visions and a human messenger to reach him.

Abraham, Moses, Hagar, both Josephs, and many others have similar stories: God communicates with them most or all of the time via intermediaries. So, although God does occasionally seem to speak and even physically appear to humans in scripture—at least as far as a literalist like me understands the text—it's much likelier, statistically speaking, that God will use some sort of go-between to get in touch with us.

Moreover, in biblical scenarios in which direct divine interaction seems irrefutable, there is often a disparity between how biblical figures characterize their experience of God's presence and what the reader is told about it. Jacob wrestles until daybreak, for example, with someone the biblical narrator refers to as simply "a man": "When the man saw that he could not overpower [Jacob], he touched the socket of Jacob's hip so that his hip was wrenched as he wrestled with the man" (Genesis 32:25). Afterward, this "man" tells Jacob, "You have struggled with God" and renames Jacob "Israel," or Struggles with God (Genesis 32:28). Jacob, for his part, names the place where he fought with the man Face of God, because, as he exclaims, "I saw God face to face, and yet my life was spared"

(Genesis 32:30). Thus, the biblical narrator's "man" transforms during the story into "God." Complicating matters further, biblical commentators often speculate that this man/God was, in fact, an angel. So, the person whom both Jacob and the man himself identify as "God" may have been an angel or a mere human. Such metamorphoses of humans or angels into God in the course of a narrative happen elsewhere in scripture, notably in the accounts of Abraham's three visitors and Hagar in the desert.

Perhaps the confusion in such passages of scripture is, in fact, the problem of God's physical body—or lack of one. Certainly, if I am right that we were made in God's bodily image, then a meeting with God might seem no different than a meeting with a fellow human being. Knowing that one had met God would depend, then, on one's interpretation of what one had seen, heard, and perhaps touched. Conceivably, when biblical prophets—or outcast servants—say, "I saw God" or "God spoke to me," they may actually be referring to a more ethereal experience of God's presence than these words suggest or else to an encounter with some sort of divine surrogate. In short, even the clearest scriptural references to God's direct intervention in people's lives suggest that, rather than come in person to deliver a message, God is likelier to appear to us or speak to us via dreams, visions, signs, and messengers. And unless we are prepared to recognize these manifestations of God's presence—indeed, unless we are on the alert for them—we may miss out on key experiences of the "God nearby" in our lives.

I have always been impressed with how Jesus' stepfather, Joseph, solved the many dilemmas that arose from his connection to Mary and her divine son by paying attention to and acting on his dreams. When he found out that the woman he was about to marry was pregnant by someone else, he resolved to break off the betrothal—

"quietly," we're told, because he was "a righteous man and did not want to expose her to public disgrace" (Matthew 1:19). The punishment among Jews for the public disgrace of having sex with someone while engaged to someone else was death by stoning (Deuteronomy 22:24). Although Joseph was a righteous man—that is, devoted to the Law—and although Mary's apparent crime surely hurt and humiliated him, his gentleness and concern on her behalf reveal the kind of righteous man he was: one who, like Jesus, valued kindness toward others over what many of their peers would have considered the letter of the law.

Joseph, in any case, lay down one night around that time and prayed and worried and yearned, and "an angel of the Lord appeared to him in a dream and said, 'Joseph son of David, do not be afraid to take Mary home as your wife, because what is conceived in her is from the Holy Spirit. She will give birth to a son, and you are to give him the name Jesus, because he will save his people from their sins'" (Matthew 1:20–21). On the strength of his dream, Joseph "did what the angel of the Lord had commanded him and took Mary home as his wife. But he had no union with her until she gave birth to a son. And he gave him the name Jesus" (Matthew 1:24–25). Later, Joseph fled to Egypt to protect Jesus from Herod's death sentence on little boys, returned to Israel after Herod's death, and finally settled his family in the safer district of Galilee—all in response to angels speaking to him through his dreams.

Everyone dreams. Nightly. My own dreams seem to comprise melted together narratives from my present and past life: strangely engaging hodgepodges uniting people I've long forgotten with the people of my life now—often, in fact, merging these past and present people to create changelings who never existed and whose actions and concerns make little sense to me after I wake up. My dreams hardly seem like messages from God about what I am to do in this or that situation I'm currently worried about. Rather, they seem to be a shuffling and sorting of recent and past memories into the various places where my brain stores them. That, in any case, is how I instinctively understand the dream process, and it's pretty close to how some scientists explain what happens when we dream.

Even if I did have a dream in which God or an angel gave me unambiguous instruction, I'm guessing I wouldn't recognize the dream as divine intervention at all. Especially if the dream instruction involved, as Joseph's did, marrying a person who I was certain had been unfaithful to me or fleeing to another country to escape a dream-divulged death sentence. Rather, I would think, *Whoa!* That *was a weird dream!* And at the breakfast table my husband and I would laugh about it.

Joseph responded to his dreams completely differently than I would have, though—and it could be that Joseph's dreams were no more comprehensible than mine. They may have been similar to the jumbles of present worries and past experiences that I dream nightly. Some of the material for Joseph's dreams was certainly available from his current circumstances. Mary had probably told him about her own visit from an angel, who, like Joseph's dream angel, had also said the boy's name would be Jesus. Joseph may have heard stories of their relative Zechariah's angel visit. And there was surely much discussion and worry among the Jews in Bethlehem and the vicinity about Herod's malice. We know that Joseph balked at the dream angel's command that he return to Israel, where the cruel son of Herod "was reigning in Judea in place of his father" (Matthew 2:22). Joseph's subsequent dream, in which he is told to return home to Galilee instead, may have derived from Joseph's own considerations of the relative safety of different places. I'm not trying to argue, here, that Joseph made up his dream instructions or that his dream was *not* a prophetic message sent directly from God. I'm merely suggesting that he may have had dreams just like mine but somehow discerned, in his righteousness, how to hear God's voice through them.

Whether Joseph's dreams were special or just like mine, though, it's clear that he read his dreams through faith. Faith in a God who he knew would not send him a wife who *seemed* as chaste and honest and devoted to God as he was but in reality slept around and lied and sought to make mock of God's promises. Faith in a God who would not abandon him and his family in their distress. Faith in a God who loved him, despite the fears and worries that undermined Joseph's courage to do as he was commanded. Joseph had faith in a God who longed to participate in his life. A God who was actively present, even as Joseph slept.

Joseph was also attentive to the presence of angels—who, as we have seen, are often interchangeable with God in biblical accounts, perhaps because angels perpetually "stand in the presence of God," as the angel Gabriel claims *he* does (Luke 1:19). Joseph, in any case, must genuinely have believed in the psalmist's promises that "If you say, 'The LORD is my refuge,'" then God "will command his angels concerning you / to guard you in all your ways" (Psalm 91:9, 11). Joseph probably *expected* God's angels to watch out for him and was less surprised than I would be to encounter incontrovertible evidence of their attendance in his life.

Sadly, although I do in some sense believe the psalmist's promise that "The angel of the LORD encamps around those who fear him" (Psalm 34:7), I would nevertheless have to force myself to actually *rely* on such a promise of protection in a real way. Faith in divine protection competes with ample evidence that believers prove as vulnerable to misfortune as anyone else. Indeed, even the most righteous people suffer and die. Throughout the Bible, God's chosen spokespeople, including the Son of God himself, are routinely hated and killed. Faith in angelic protection—that is, faith in God's presence in one's life in the form of angels—demands, however, that one trust such promises despite evidence to the contrary. Which is hard, so hard, to do.

One of my favorite Bible stories—and one of the funniest—illustrates particularly well the difficulty involved in believing in angels. In the story, "the angel of the LORD" visits a barren woman—which happens a lot in scripture—and tells her that she's pregnant (Judges 13:3). Her son is to be "a Nazirite, dedicated to God from the womb" (Judges 13:5), so the angel gives her strict instructions regarding what she must do to insure that all goes according to plan: She must not drink alcohol or eat anything unclean, and her son's hair must never be cut.

The woman then goes to her husband, Manoah, and tells him, "A man of God came to me. He looked like an angel of God, very awesome. I didn't ask him where he came from, and he didn't tell me his name" (Judges 13:6). Although the reader knows that this "man of God" the woman refers to really *is* an angel, the woman is not entirely sure. He may have *looked* like an angel of God, as she says, but she reports her encounter as she might an encounter with an ordinary person—just exactly as I might tell my own husband about a similar encounter with some stranger out in one of our fields. "This guy came up to me out in that field north of the road and was saying all kinds of crazy stuff. Kind of good looking, in an androgynous sort of way. Looked like an angel or something. Dang! I forgot to ask his name!"

Anyway, after the woman summarizes the angel's instructions, Manoah prays to the Lord that what he also calls "the man of God" will return and give them more precise parenting advice. God answers him by sending the angel out in the field to Manoah's wife again. This time, she leaves the angel there—seemingly trusting that he'll still be there, as a regular person would be, when she gets back—and runs to tell her husband, "He's here! The man who appeared to me the other day!" (Judges 13:10). The "man of God" who looks like an "angel of God" is now just a "man," which is also what Manoah calls him when he follows his wife back to the place where she saw him and demands, "Are you the man who talked to my wife?" (Judges 13:11). He sounds kind of miffed to me, as I suppose my husband might be if some awesome-looking guy had been chatting me up out in our fields. Manoah asks for details on how the boy is to be raised, but the angel only repeats the advice he has already given.

Manoah then invites the angel to a dinner of young goat, but the angel declines, suggesting that the couple instead make a burnt offering to the Lord. When they do this, we're told that

> the LORD did an amazing thing while Manoah and his wife watched: As the flame blazed up from the altar toward heaven, the angel of the LORD ascended in the flame. Seeing this, Manoah and his wife fell with their faces to the ground. When the angel of the LORD did not show himself again to Manoah and his wife, Manoah realized that it was the angel of the LORD.
>
> "We are doomed to die!" he said to his wife. "We have seen God!"
>
> But his wife answered, "If the LORD had meant to kill us, he would not have accepted a burnt offering and grain offering from our hands, nor shown us all these things or now told us this." (Judges 13:19–23)

The story offers considerable evidence that the person the couple are dealing with is no ordinary man. He looks "awesome" and, although a stranger to the couple, knows that the woman is barren, predicts both the pregnancy and the gender of the unborn child, and gives them commands concerning the boy's future. The couple are clearly devoted to God, as evidenced by Manoah's prayer, the sacrifice, the interpretation of their vision as being from God, and the wife's final assertion about God's nature and will. Nevertheless, until the couple's final "amazing" experience with the man, they are unaware that they've actually been conversing with an angel. Indeed, they seem to outright resist believing in angels. Once they can get their minds around the fact that the man *is* an angel, though, their immediate response is, "We have seen God!" It takes an "amazing thing" from God and considerable effort on the couple's part to make them truly understand that they've been the whole while in the presence of God.

Realizing one is in the presence of an angel, like realizing one is in the presence of God, is an act of will. In a passage from Marilynne Robinson's novel *Gilead*,[2] the main character, an elderly pastor facing his death and reflecting on his life in a long letter to his young son, offers an engaging strategy for how to be on the alert for angels. Whenever you have dealings with someone, he advises his son—especially unpleasant dealings—you should consider what God might be demanding of you in that situation. Rather than act the same way the person acts toward you, you might instead regard the person as a messenger from God whose visit will in some way benefit you. Looking at others as God's emissaries, the pastor counsels, frees one from responding automatically or in kind. It also invites one, I would argue, into the presence of God.

Don't misunderstand me. I am not saying that everyone you meet is an angel or that angels and people are the same thing. Although the etymology of the word *angel*, in English as in the Hebrew and Greek of the Bible, is simply "messenger," it is nevertheless clear from many scriptural accounts that God's angels are *not* human beings but another sort of being altogether. That said, viewing others as God's messengers makes you aware of God as the choreographer of your daily encounters. Thus, whether you sense it or not, God is physically present, if only by proxy, whenever you are in the company of others.

There's certainly no harm in regarding others as stand-ins for God. Indeed, Jesus does so himself. In addressing the question, "Which is the greatest commandment in the Law?" he boils down "All the Law and the Prophets"—that is, the entirety of scripture in his day—to two rules that he describes as "like" each other: "Love the Lord your God with all your heart and with all your soul and with all your mind" and "Love your neighbor as yourself" (Matthew 22:36–40). In other words, by loving others, we love God.

Viewing others as God's proxies—that is, as potential angels—also obliges one to take seriously biblical promises of angels surrounding believers and looking after their interests. Then, if it should happen that one has the good fortune of encountering a real angel, one is prepared to say, along with Manoah and his wife and Hagar and Jacob and others, "I have seen God!"

You may want to refrain from actually saying that, however. Announcements of supernatural experiences such as angel visits, visions, and prophetic dreams often meet with disapproval nowadays, for one thing. People either don't believe you, or they think you are bragging about your own godliness, or else they envy you and feel slighted by God that they haven't had similar experiences.

Also, proclaiming your otherworldly experience of God has the effect of focusing attention on the otherworldliness, rather than on God. Scripture offers many accounts of false prophets who go around claiming to have had visions and dreams, and, although biblical writers often mention their own dreams and visions, they warn against relying on such claims of others or making them oneself. Jeremiah writes, in the voice of God,

> I have heard what the prophets say who prophesy lies in my name. They say, "I had a dream! I had a dream!" How long will this continue in the hearts of these lying prophets, who prophesy the delusions of their own minds? They think the dreams they tell one another will make my people forget my name, just as their ancestors forgot my name through Baal worship. (Jeremiah 23:25–27)

Experiencing God through dreams, visions, amazing signs, and encounters with angels is a very special and intimate way of enjoying God's company—best savored, perhaps, in private. Like the intimate details of a sexual relationship, supernatural experiences of God are rarely appropriate material for public enjoyment or even edification.

That said, I can't resist recounting a vision I had many times as a young child, when I experienced God's presence routinely, without seeking it or even thinking to value it. It was during the Mass, right after Communion, when, having finished up at the altar, the priests and deacons sat down for a period of silence in throne-like chairs lined up against the wall off to one side of the altar. They all bowed their heads. They could have been praying or merely resting before the last segments of the Mass. I wasn't sure. The parishioners sat silent with their heads bowed too—also praying or resting, I supposed—but I couldn't resist watching those priests in their funny robes. Sometimes the air above one or the other of them seemed to quiver and pulse. It's hard for me to describe what I saw. A movement of sorts, like the simultaneous rising and falling of the invisible air. Or a wrinkling, as of heat rising from the asphalt when I looked down my street on a hot summer day. In any case, whenever I saw it happen, I knew I was witnessing a communication between that person and God, and I felt in the presence of something uncommonly holy.

Exercises for Paying Attention to Dreams

1 ❧ Develop a habit of paying attention to your dreams by recording them on a regular basis. Write down what happened in the dream and what your emotions were relevant to the events. (Note: If you have trouble remembering your dreams, try using autosuggestion: Just before you go to sleep, concentrate on something in your bedroom that you know you will see first thing in the morning—such as a ceiling fan, the window you keep cracked in the night, or a doorknob. Tell yourself that when you see that object upon waking up, you will recall the dream you just had. Regular practice of this technique will steadily improve your ability to remember your dreams, as will getting in the habit of recording them.)

2 ❧ Once you have gotten in the habit of paying attention to your dreams, begin to look for meaning in them. There are many popular strategies for interpreting dreams, but the one that I think best serves the purpose of seeking God's presence in your life is to simply ask yourself what you think the dream might have meant. Sometimes you may have a strong sense of what God might be saying to you through your dream, in which case, record it. Other times, your dream will be a mishmash.

3 ❧ Once you have recorded a number of dreams, read through what you have written and write down anything you notice about the dreams as a group. Are there any patterns in them—recurrent images, dominant emotions? Does a particular person figure in them often? It is not uncommon for a plot to repeat itself with different details in the course of a dream or for you to have several dreams in the course of a night with approximately the same plot. Pay attention, especially, to any connections between your current worries and the events of your dreams.

Exercises for Being on the Alert for Angels

4 ❧ Look up the word *angel* in a Bible concordance to locate angel episodes in the Bible and read them. What kinds of things typically happen when a person interacts with an angel? In what ways does the angel seem to be acting in the person's interest?

5 ❧ One thing that might be said of angel encounters in scripture is that the angel is always a stranger. Rethink several encounters with strangers as instances in which God's messengers might have been sent to you for your spiritual benefit or protection. What might that benefit or protection have been?

6 ❧ Pick a problematic person in your life whom you encounter on a regular basis and designate him or her, in your mind, as an angel whom God sent into your life for divine reasons. God may want to grow or teach or protect or perhaps simply delight you through this person. Resolve, from now on, to draw some spiritual benefit from this person's interaction with you.

7 ❧ Following the hospitality mandates of biblical times, people in the Bible who are visited by angels often offer to cook a meal for them. Practicing hospitality toward new acquaintances in your life—such as new co-workers, neighbors, fellow parents you meet through your children—is a good way of being on the alert for angels or people that God may have sent into your life for a reason.

Exercises for Acknowledging Visions and Signs

8 ❧ For the purposes of this exercise, imagine that visions and signs are nothing more elaborate than the coincidences of daily living. Not necessarily actual experiences of the supernatural in our natural world, but simply strange imaginings or occurrences that seem to mean something larger—situations that cause one to say something like, "Whoa, what's up with that?" While I was writing this book, it often happened that, having looked something up in my big concordance, I reached over for my Bible to look up the passage and opened right to the page. Similarly, because I live out in the country and have only satellite access to the Internet, I often lose my connection when it rains, and I don't know how many times I have sat before a blank screen at some crucial point in the writing process and, although nothing else will connect, watched the Web page I need materialize before my eyes. Afterward, thinking I must now have a connection, I try to check my e-mail or the news headlines. In vain. If you are like me, you witness similar "signs and visions" all the time but dismiss them as coincidences.

Use the following strategy to retool your automatic dismissal of such signs and visions into a response more receptive to the presence of God: Cut a small piece of cardstock to the size of a business card. On one side write your typical response in words you would actually use to tell someone else about the coincidence, such as "Isn't that weird?!" On the other side, write a sentence—or use a scriptural one—that reminds you that such seeming coincidences could, in fact, be evidence of a watchful God who longs to participate in your life. Carry the card with you in a place where you are likely to have it at hand most of the time. Whenever you find yourself saying the words on the one side of the card—"That's so strange!"—get the card out, flip it to the other side, and read aloud the words you have written there that affirm God's abiding presence and attention. Remember, believing, John says, is work, and work is not something that just happens on its own. It takes intentional effort, and practice.

CHAPTER ELEVEN

God's Presence in Prayer

IN MY YEARS as a nonbeliever, I felt God's absence most deeply in the beginning, when I still prayed. Indeed, you might say that my atheism developed out of a consciousness of not being heard when I prayed. The God I had known from childhood was no longer listening to me, I reasoned, and thus had either abandoned me or else had been a creation of my imagination and had never existed in the first place.

Not that I had ever enjoyed a direct response to my prayers or really noticed God's attention before it disappeared. Growing up, I never shouted, as my daughters have, "Answered prayer!" It never occurred to me to *expect* God to answer my prayers. Nevertheless, I prayed regularly as a child, and I knew—or was in the habit of believing, as I explained it to myself after I lost my faith—that God was watching and listening to me all the time. And then, God wasn't anymore.

My prayer habits before God disappeared may have set me up for this absence to some extent. I was raised in the Catholic tradition, so almost all the prayers I'd prayed as a child had been composed by someone else. Although I sometimes prayed these set prayers fervently and with great intentions of speaking my heart, my primary participation in them was to memorize and recite them. I prayed the words almost without thinking—and largely because doing so was expected of me—and certainly without actually considering that I was talking to God or that God might say something to me in return.

As soon as I could talk, I obediently "said my prayers" every night before I went to sleep, using a Catholic child's bedtime prayer common in those days:

> Angel of God, my guardian dear,
> To whom God's love entrusts me here,
> Ever this day be at my side,
> To light, to guard, to rule and guide, amen.

As I prayed, I felt myself guarded, through God's love, by an invisible angel, but I never paid any attention at all to the prayer's explicit plea for governance and guidance. I probably didn't desire such supervision then—angelic or otherwise—although I surely needed it. My prayer was, thus, not so much a communication with God—or even with the angel to whom the prayer was addressed—as it was a confirmation of what I believed as a child: namely, that God loved me and had assigned me an angel as my personal escort.

Some of the prayers I prayed made no impression on me whatsoever. Long before I ever knew what the word *bounty* meant, I joined my family nightly in the traditional Catholic blessing before dinner: "Bless us, oh Lord, for these thy gifts which we are about to receive through Thy bounty, through Christ our Lord, amen." It was a jumble of words whose only purpose seemed to be to postpone the meal by the few seconds it took us to say them. I felt no thanks, not the least consciousness of the amazing bounty I had enjoyed from birth in the comfortable suburban neighborhoods where my family lived. My first inkling of God's bounteous provision would come to me only later, in adulthood, after I had lived for a while on a graduate student stipend of $315 a month, eaten beans daily for months at a time, and yearned all week long for my Friday feast of one Popeyes spicy chicken breast and a biscuit. Even that grad school inkling of what *bounty* meant deepened to genuine appreciation only after I had lived in places where others survived, gratefully, on much, much less.

I needed to see, when I lived in China, women washing clothes in holes in the concrete outside the single-room boxes they and their extended families called home. And to sense behind me, in the dumpling restaurants I frequented, old people lurking, willing me to finish up quickly so that they could glean any edible scraps I left behind. I needed to hear the rasping wail, throughout the long hot night, of the newborn child of the hardworking couple who lived next door to me in one of a string of cheap apartments I rented in Hong Kong; for lack of room or quiet or alternatives to a life of danger utterly foreign to me, they kept the little wisp of helplessness in a box on our shared stairwell landing. I couldn't really pray gratitude for bounty, in other words, until I had witnessed its opposite: penury.

Similarly, in church every Sunday growing up, I orally reviewed the foundations of my faith in prayers I can still recite word for word— the Creed, the Gloria, the Lord Have Mercy—but I never really examined the faith they described until after I had struggled to understand its tenets half a lifetime later.

I'm not saying that all the habitual prayers of my faith were utterly meaningless to me, even in childhood. During the Mass, I was always mysteriously moved by a humble appeal—borrowed from the story of the Roman centurion in the gospels, although I didn't know that then—that congregants offered before Communion: "Lord, I am not worthy that Thou shouldst enter under my roof, but only say the word and my soul shall be healed." I was also regularly tickled by the final prayer of the service, when the priest gave his standard dismissal— "The Mass is ended. Go in peace to love and serve the Lord"—and we all joyously responded, "Thanks be to God!" And in the Confession booth, I prayed—and sincerely meant—the Act of Contrition, a prayer that to this day surfaces from the depths of my memory whenever I feel remorse:

> O my God, I am heartily sorry for having offended Thee, and I detest all my sins because of Thy just punishments, but most of all because they offend Thee, my God, Who art all good and deserving of all my love. I firmly resolve, with the help of Thy grace, to sin no more and to avoid near occasions of sin. Amen.

Despite these sporadic instances of attention to the words in my mouth, though, I rarely consciously considered what I was praying. In fact, when one of the set prayers of my childhood reappears nowadays, as often happens at the traditional Presbyterian church I currently attend, I'm often alarmed by what I'm saying. *Where in scripture does it say Jesus went to hell during his three days in the grave?* I wonder as we pray the Apostles' Creed. Midprayer, I suddenly decide that, since I don't know the answer to my question, then I can't *mean* those words, and therefore I can't speak them. When I fall silent mid-Creed, my daughters look over at me questioningly—and, I suspect, a bit accusingly—and I long, for their sake, to join back in with the voices of our fellow believers. But not only would praying words I didn't believe be a lie of the worst kind, one told for the sake of fitting in, but it would also be what I think of these days as "unprayer": a communication that I suspect God doesn't give a rip about and to which I don't really expect a response. A little rumble of holy noise uttered for no other purpose than to affect a devotion I don't really feel.

My definition of prayer these days is the opposite of unprayer. Prayer is *not* a statement of the tenets of my faith. Not even when I can wholeheartedly affirm what it is I'm saying. Prayer, in my view, is too much of a shared experience—too interpersonal in its intentions —to be a mere pronouncement of my beliefs, in which God merely listens and plays no role. On the other hand, prayer is also *not* a conversation, exactly, although it does involve a genuine communication on my part to which I desire a response. Rather, prayer is a direct invocation and acknowledgment of God's presence. When I pray, I am asserting—to myself and to God—that God is with me. Right now. And paying attention.

God's participation in my prayer—God's response, if you will— is, as I see it, pretty much what my daughters have always expected of me whenever they want to tell me something or whenever they feel hurt or angry or affectionate: that I be fully present. I'm not particularly good at being fully present to them—one of the many sins that give rise to those involuntary Acts of Contrition. Although I love my daughters more than anything in the world, I am a terrible listener. When Lulu was a toddler, she used to grab my face and hold onto it when she had something to say. And once, when she was maybe seven or eight, she made me a list of exactly what she wanted me to do and not do whenever she was talking to me. I was to look her directly in the face. I was not to do anything else while she was talking. I was not to respond with *uh-hm* or any other habitual nonlistening noise. I was not to interrupt. And, afterward, I was not to forget anything she said. She wanted—and, as a teenager, still wants—my full and abiding attention.

Call me demanding or codependent. Accuse me of having a dou-
ble standard, since I am such a poor listener myself. But Lulu's list is
what I expect of God. When I pray, although I may secretly hope to
hear God's actual voice or to witness specific actions in response to
my prayer, what I want most is to know that God cares about what
I'm saying. Because *I* care about what I'm saying. Prayer, in other
words, is giving voice to something that one cares about deeply with
the expectation that God is listening and cares too.

When I first became a believer as an adult, I felt like a complete
failure in the area of prayer. The set prayers of my childhood, for one
thing, did not prepare me for the spontaneous prayers offered in the
churches I started visiting in adulthood. Not, mind you, that I
thought then or think now that precomposed prayers are somehow
wrong—or immature or less valuable—than the prayers one makes up
as one goes. Both sorts of prayer can be unprayer, offered up, often
in the presence of others, merely because one is *supposed* to be praying.
Both can also be genuine attempts to enter God's presence. That said,
spontaneous prayer is definitely a learned skill, one in which every
other believer I encountered in those days seemed dauntingly gifted.
Whenever *I* tried to pray aloud without carefully planning what I had
to say, I invariably stumbled over my words, started crying, or committed the mortal sin of public prayer: contradicting or altering what
had already been said. Even praying silently didn't work for me. I got
distracted.

Worse, although I *wanted* to pray and I believed by then that God
was listening and *did* care about what I had to say, somehow my prayers
still felt vacant. Or false, somehow. I couldn't pray, I decided.

In the Christian community in which I found myself, though,
there was considerable pressure to pray—all the time and about
matters I would never have thought of praying about. Prayer was the

commentary upon even the most minor items of news and the punctuation of all activities. In church services and before meetings at my Christian university and even sometimes in class, we totted up long lists of others' "needs and praises" and prayed through them, one by one. True Christians prayed before *all* meals, I learned, not just before supper with the family. My colleagues and students lowered their heads in the school cafeteria and prayed silently over their veggie wraps and curly fries before joining the ongoing conversation. Fellow faculty and staff signed off even the most mundane business e-mails with some sort of cheery benediction or statement of faith or faith-provoking quote, often in a special font clearly intended to look more spiritual than the Arial 10 used in the body of the message. *Blessings. In Christ. Proverbs 14:15: "A simple man believes anything, but a prudent man gives thought to his steps."* From one friend, I routinely received e-mails that ended, "*. . . greed is the hatred of mercy,*" a quote from Wendell Berry,[1] and I worried that my friend thought me especially covetous and mean. Certain of my growing Christian acquaintance were referred to as "prayer warriors," a term I found impressive, although somewhat scary. I imagined them hunched low on their knees, like soldiers in stealthy combat, advancing night and day through endless lists of prayer requests, and I tried to motivate myself to emulate them. In vain.

To be honest, most of the time I didn't really care about the needs and praises for which I knew I was supposed to be praying. I just couldn't get agitated enough about others' traveling mercies, bad colds, losses of grandparents, and marriage engagements to pray a prayer that felt real. If someone's news was particularly spectacular— a cancer diagnosis, say, or a bad car accident or a tornado—I had a better chance of getting into it. About the only time I prayed for others and really meant it, though, was when, having volunteered or been asked to pray, I *forgot* someone on the list, as I inevitably did, and then remembered it much later, after everyone was gone. Embarrassment and remorse enlivened my pleas on that person's behalf: *Dear Father*, I prayed, *let them not think I didn't care. Oh, and let the family be comforted*—or the house be sold or whatever it was that I had neglected.

Even my own concerns were hard to pray about on demand. When I prayed before an audience, I was always hyperconscious of what I sounded like. And when I prayed in private, I worried about how self-centered my prayers were compared to the selfless prayers I knew I *should* be praying.

Indeed, prayer in those days was all about *should*. Somehow, in the first years of my adult faith, prayer became a spiritual duty—and, secretly, often an irritating one—rather than the comforting habit it had been in my childhood or the pleasure and relief it is to me nowadays. Like most spiritual duties, prayer was something I could never get quite right. *What am I doing wrong?* I wondered, and I questioned Christian friends and pastors about how they prayed. Some of them had impressive prayer habits and certainty about what prayer was supposed to be like. One friend told me prayer was simply sharing fellowship with God. She had early morning devotionals for which she brewed two cups of tea, one for her and one for God. Another friend said prayer was not about speaking but about being silent and listening. Several people I knew went on enviable prayer retreats to far off holy places, like Iona, off the coast of Scotland, and the Greek island of Athos. Others wore little black cord bracelets to remind themselves to pray constantly. My own husband prayed, on his knees, in our walk-in closet.

Most of my acquaintance, though, were too embarrassed about their prayer habits to give me any details, and many confessed to discontent similar to mine. Either they didn't pray enough or about the right things, they hinted, or else they suspected, as I did, that there was some *right* way to pray that they had yet to discover. In this we shared Jesus' disciples' bafflement about prayer, evident in their recorded prayer failures—such as falling asleep instead of praying in Jesus' hour of need in Gethsemane—and in their plea that Jesus teach them *how* to pray.

It's such an odd request, when you think about it. Surely, talking about what you care about to someone you love ought to come naturally. As young children, we don't have to be taught how to wail when we are hurt or to cuddle when we feel affectionate. In marriage, we tell our excitements and concerns to our spouses without planning, without thinking too much about how to say whatever it is or worrying about getting it right.

And the disciples must have been fairly experienced in the area of prayer. They had undoubtedly participated in all sorts of corporate and private prayer and witnessed Jesus praying on many occasions, and they had been present for his numerous sermons on prayer. Don't pray like the hypocrites, he told them. Don't pray lengthy prayers or repeat yourself ad nauseam. Pray in secret. Don't pray ostentatiously. If the disciples were like me, they probably recognized themselves in the examples Jesus offered for how *not* to pray. *Am I like that idiotic Pharisee?* they fretted. *A fake?* On one occasion, the disciples couldn't cast out a demon that caused a boy to have convulsions and foam at the mouth. Jesus simply commanded the demon to leave the boy and it did, but when the disciples wanted to know what they'd done wrong, he told them, "This kind can come out only by prayer" (Mark 9:29)—as though that explained everything.

Jesus made prayer sound so simple: "You may ask me for anything in my name," he told his disciples, "and I will do it" (John 14:14). Perhaps the disciples had tried out this prayer recipe—

I know I have!—and it didn't seem to work. In any case, the disciples probably worried, just as I have worried, that they didn't pray selflessly enough or often enough or about the right sort of things. Like me, they considered themselves failures when it came to prayer.

"Lord, teach us to pray, just as John taught his disciples," one of them eventually begged outright (Luke 11:1), unaware that his very request *was* a prayer.

As my faith matured, my inability to pray—or, that is, my inability to pray and feel good about it—continued, until finally, many years into my faith, I received an e-mail that changed my whole way of looking at prayer. It came from a former creative writing student of mine who had struggled mightily for years against drugs and despair. He couldn't go to church, couldn't pray, and, last I'd heard, had stopped believing in God entirely. In his e-mail, he told me that he had finally gotten himself onto more stable ground. His personal life was shaping up, he said, and his faith was slowly returning. He had also started writing again—"weird little devotional essays," he said, like the ones I wrote that he remembered me reading aloud in class.

"Does it ever seem to you that your writing *is* prayer?" he asked.

His question was transformational. Afterward, I felt as though this struggling young believer *gave* me prayer—not just the prayers I prayed subsequently as weird little devotional essays, but all the other prayers I'd been praying all along. The self-centered, almost unconscious pleas for help I sent up to my invisible Creator and Parent and Guide whenever I was in trouble; my botched efforts to pray through lists of others' needs; and even the set prayers I mouthed with my fellow believers at church—including the ones I was unable to join in on—were all efforts to acknowledge God's presence. They were all, in other words, prayer. Failed prayer, yes. God knows my prayers were vain at times, ridiculous at others, always inadequate for the circumstances, and at best mere mindless moans.

The apostle Paul points out, "we do not know how to pray as we ought" (Romans 8:26 NRSV). The most effectual prayer of even the most devout believer, he says, amounts to little more than "groaning in labor pains" along with the rest of creation (Romans 8:22 NRSV). But, Paul reassures us, "the Spirit helps us in our weakness" by interceding for us with "sighs too deep for words. And God, who searches the heart, knows what is the mind of the Spirit" (Romans 8:26–27 NRSV).

It seems strange to me that Jesus, who had so much to say on the subject of prayer, left it to Paul to offer us this encouragement. When the disciples asked Jesus how to pray, the answer he gave them—the words of which became the formulaic prayer that even believers who reject formulaic prayers often recite—suggests, if anything, that there *might actually be* a learnable right way to pray: We should pray that God will take care of us and forgive us and lead us away from what tempts us, and, above all, we should pray that God's will, not ours, be carried out. Sadly, these worthy prayer requests are rarely the ones I put before God, unless I'm actually reciting—whether at church or privately, as I often do before big decisions—Jesus' model prayer, which I have known from childhood as "the Our Father."

The straightforward prayer advice Jesus offered on another occasion heartens me, though: "Whatever you ask for in prayer, believe that you have received it, and it will be yours" (Mark 11:24). Interestingly, he doesn't say, "believe that you *will receive* it" but rather "believe that you *have received* it." The difference in tense is vast in its implications. Essentially, Jesus is inviting us to approach prayer neither as a duty nor as a holy habit but as an opportunity to trust and be reassured that God is not only paying attention to us when we pray but has been paying attention to us all along.

And that is the answer Jesus offers to the prayer I have prayed nonstop since becoming a believer, which is the same prayer Jesus' disciples unwittingly prayed in asking Jesus to teach them all how to pray—the prayer, namely, to be able to communicate effectively with our unseen, unheard, untouchable God. In the asking, Jesus says, we have already received what we desire, even if we don't yet know it.

God hears, and responds to, every prayer. Even if we pray badly. Even if we are so self-centered that we can only pray for our own needs. Even if we pray without really believing that God is listening. Even if we pray without being sure that God is there at all.

God hears, Jesus assures us, even when we pray without knowing we are praying. Newborns cry because they are born with the expectation that their needs will be met, that their pains and fears will be comforted. They are born, in other words, instinctively praying forth their confidence in God's initial promises of food, comfort, one another. And God is right there with that baby, listening to and caring about each small wail—especially when those wails don't move any humans to address the child's needs, as, sadly, happens all too often in our broken world.

The typical life is full of groaning. Full of prayers. In my case, I do my groaning in essays that come over me entirely unbidden and detail my ongoing struggle to love and understand the God I worship. I am praying when I cry, as I often do, about others' victimization. And when I rage over injustice. And when, in despondency, I long for heaven. When I seek the counsel of more knowledgeable believers in my spiritual struggles, I am praying. And, despite some believers' view that worrying is sin, I am praying whenever I worry on others' or even my own behalf. (I call this kind of prayer "pray-worrying.") My student's e-mail invited me to regard all of these accidental prayers and many others as opportunities to acknowledge, in retrospect, God's imperceptible presence and attention.

My student's comment also spurred me to claim these and other communications with God in my daily life not merely by acknowledging them as prayer but by praying them forth more intentionally as invitations for God to join me. Increasingly, my longing, my worries, my thankfulness for the amazing bounty I enjoy, and even my frequent frustration and anger with our messed up world have become areas of my life in which I experience God's presence most intimately. Listening to my own prayers, I sense God listening too—now mourning with me, now agreeing, now hoping I will see things another way, but always looking directly into my face, not interrupting, not saying anything, not making any sound at all, but just breathing my prayer in, like air. In such moments, the most essential prayer that underlies all prayers—the prayer for God's company—has, in the praying, already been answered.

I ❧ The Psalms are prayers. If you examine them, you will find that most of them are about events—often unpleasant ones—from the psalmist's life. In these prayers, the psalmist routinely complains, worries, whines, and begs God to be present. By the end of the psalm, though, the psalmist typically affirms the abiding presence of God—sometimes offering evidence—and the confidence that the problems mentioned have been addressed. The Psalms are, in other words, models of the sort of praying Jesus recommended to his disciples, in which one believes that one's prayer has already been answered. Read a few psalms and select one to use as a model for your own about some problem in your own life. Substitute your own worries and complaints for those of the psalmist and search your life for your own evidence that your prayer has already been answered. Be as concrete as you can, both in describing your issue and in affirming God's attention to the matter.

2 ❧ In downtown Dallas, on a little triangle of public space called Thanks-Giving Square, sits the beautiful little Chapel of Thanksgiving, a coiled concrete building topped with an ascending spiral of stained glass that serves as an interfaith shrine to the universal human urge to give thanks. I learned about the chapel's existence after a depressed and religion-hostile friend, overwhelmed with thankfulness for finally finding a good job after a multiyear search, happened upon it and deposited in the chapel's glass Prayer Bowl a card expressing her gratitude and relief. Set out your own prayer bowl—perhaps to celebrate a birthday or anniversary or Thanksgiving—in which to collect your and your guests' thanks and thereby invite God into your collective company.

3 ❧ When Charlotte was little and I used to clean her room, I often found under her pillow or on her desk little scraps of paper rolled up into tiny scrolls and tied with bits of colored thread. I should have honored her privacy, probably, but I couldn't resist unrolling and reading them. Sometimes they were little scriptural passages with which she was admonishing herself, like "Do not be afraid; do not be discouraged, for the LORD your God will be with you wherever you go" (Joshua 1:9). Other times they were prayer requests in her own words. What always

impressed me was the pomp with which she offered up these prayers: the careful handwriting, usually in a colored pen that matched the thread; the rolling up of the paper; the tininess of the scroll, which made it seem the more precious. When Charlotte got older and started keeping a diary, she went through phases when she began entries with an excerpt from scripture. Make a small formal ritual of your own for offering up prayer in a special way. Alternatively, incorporate scripture into some routine record you regularly keep, such as a dietary or exercise account or a desk calendar.

4 ❧ Experiment with different types of prayer than the ones you usually employ. If you are in the habit of freeform prayer, try out various forms of composed prayer. Use the Internet to find composed prayers—perhaps of another denomination or even another faith—that might house your own thoughts. Pray the prayer of someone in scripture, such as the father in Mark 9:24 NRSV, who wanted Jesus to heal his son's seizures but struggled to believe Jesus really could and prayed, "Help my unbelief!" Pray forth a passage of scripture that has meaning for you. Try repeating just one line of a longer prayer, such as "Thy will be done." Alternatively, write down and memorize your own prayers to use and reuse on specific occasions.

5 ❧ Intercessory prayer has always been difficult for me. I tend to forget others' prayer needs and, deep down, not care about them as much as I do my own. I also struggle to see problems from others' points of view. Serendipitously, solving a prayer problem in my advanced grammar course helped me experience prayer for others in a new way. Many students struggle academically in that class, and some take great comfort in praying communally before important tests. Others, however, don't like to lose a second of the allotted time. To address their conflicting needs on the final exam, I routinely compose a prayer on my students' behalf and affix it to the test for them to read, or not, at their leisure. In this way, I pray long in advance of their need. Also, my prayer shapes the way I see the test while it's still in the making. I always find myself newly aware of my students and their struggles when I pray in this way. My students not only appreciate the prayer but say it helps them see their own situation through my eyes. Try composing a written prayer for another in advance of an upcoming difficulty and then share it with that person.

CHAPTER TWELVE

Miracles, Gifts, and Other Good Things

THE OTHER DAY I attended one of our university chapel services, and a visiting preacher—Brennan Manning, author of *The Ragamuffin Gospel*—gave a sermon against self-hatred.[1] He argued that the most important and, for many, the most difficult requirement of faith is allowing oneself to *be loved* by God.

He asked us to close our eyes and imagine Jesus walking up to the front of the chapel and looking out across the pews directly at us. Then he asked us, "What is Jesus' face saying to you?"

Many of us, Manning predicted, would see Jesus looking stern or accusing. What we *should* see, Manning coached, was a loving look— the gaze of one utterly enthralled with what he saw. Jesus should be looking at us the way a parent would look at a cherished child.

The Jesus I imagined did not regard me as he would a beloved daughter—or a beloved sister, which I thought a more apt analogy. Nor did he regard me with sternness or condemnation. Rather, he looked over at me with surprise, his eyebrows raised, as though to ask, "What are *you* doing here?"

It was the same look I imagined him giving that Canaanite woman who wanted him to heal her demon-possessed daughter. He ignored her pleas for so long that it caused a scene and his disciples begged him to send her away. He didn't. Instead, he explained to her that he "was sent only to the lost sheep of Israel" and that "It is not right to take the children's bread and toss it to the dogs" (Matthew 15:24, 26). Only after the woman's gutsy retort that even dogs get to lick up the crumbs of the children's meal did Jesus finally relent and heal her daughter.

"What's a dog like you doing here?" Jesus' surprised expression said to me. All day long, I lamented my vision and pondered what it might mean. *Was it my lifelong sense of being an outsider*, I wondered, *getting in the way of my letting God love me? Was it some unconscious suspicion, underlying the confident faith I professed, that God was primarily interested in churchy people, not spiritual individualists like me?*

Seeing God as someone who loves me just as I am is a hard place to get to—especially in the context of a church service, where sermons and songs so often focus on the necessity of being *better* than I am. Countless biblical accounts—certainly the various destructions, such as the Flood, Sodom and Gomorrah, and the instantaneous deaths of Aaron's sons and the deceitful couple, Ananias and Sapphira—seem to support the view that God only likes us when we do the right thing. And I am such a failure at doing the right thing.

I thought about how Jesus depicted God's love, though. There's God as the prodigal dad, who lets his obnoxious younger son blow his inheritance and then, after the son repents, dresses the greedy schmuck up in fancy clothes, puts a ring on his finger, and throws a big party, pooh-poohing the objections of his dutiful, hardworking elder son.

In another analogy, Jesus portrays God as the friend whose door you pound on in the middle of the night to get three loaves of bread for a departing guest.

"I tell you," Jesus explains, "even though he will not get up and give you the bread because of friendship, yet because of your shameless audacity he will surely get up and give you as much as you need" (Luke 11:8).

A bit later in the same discourse, Jesus compares God to earthly parents: "Which of you fathers, if your son asks for a fish, will give him a snake instead? Or if he asks for an egg, will give him a scorpion?" (Luke 11:11–12).

The God Jesus is talking about in these stories gives in to rash and even sinful demands—such as demanding an inheritance prematurely, which amounts to wishing the father dead—and loves humans just as irrationally as we love our children. Despite their self-centeredness. Despite their mistakes and even their deliberate misconduct. Despite their teenage anger and self-indulgence. Despite frequent lapses in their own love. According to Jesus, God loves us enough to acquiesce to some pretty unreasonable pleas, as most parents probably do. And, like any parent, God longs to give us good things.

I thought about how I would look at Charlotte and Lulu across that chapel, with what love and pride and delight, even though I would be as surprised and vexed to see them at my university—at 10:30 on a Tuesday morning, when they were supposed to be in school!—as Jesus was to see *me* in my imagined encounter.

I'm foolishly in love with my daughters. I find it difficult to say no to their desires, however frivolous. Although I'm frugal almost to the point of having a disability, I love to buy things I think will please them. Crazy things, expensive things, things I would never think of buying for myself. Jewelry that lights up. Toys I longed for and never got as a child. Delicate, diaphanous panties a queen might wear. The other day I bought Lulu, who loves bananas, a tiny bunch of miniature bananas, each no bigger than my pinky, that cost five times as much as a single regular banana—not for their nutritional or even gustatory value but just because they were so cute and I knew they would delight her. When I'm mad at one of my daughters, when we're right in the middle of a fight, I find myself gazing at her with dopey fondness. *God's like that*, I spent the afternoon after chapel trying to convince myself, *only more so. God loves me more than I am capable of loving my daughters. More crazily.*

Later that evening, in one of the coincidences I've come to expect whenever I'm in the grip of some new revelation about God, one of my colleagues gave a dinner lecture on "servant-leadership" and acquainted me with the writings of Robert K. Greenleaf, who coined the term back in 1970.[2] Greenleaf, I discovered, said that to be a good leader, one must first learn not only how to serve others, but, as counterintuitive as the idea might seem, how to *be served* by others. Evidently, at least according to Greenleaf, allowing oneself to *be* served, like allowing oneself to *be* loved by God, does not come without effort. One has to learn it.

Nowhere is the difficulty of allowing oneself to be loved by God more apparent, I think, than in believers' reluctance to ask for miracles. Think of what, in your most shameless audacity, you might ask of God. For the healing of a loved one's incurable illness. For the turning back of time after a devastating disaster. For an unequivocal sign of God's invisible presence when you are suffering uncertainty or loneliness or despair. If you're like me, you can barely allow yourself to hope for, much less actually request, such impossible boons in your conversations with God. But try. Imagine yourself pounding on God's door, demanding a favor you wouldn't ask of your closest friend. And imagine God—watery-eyed, in rumpled pajamas, surprised and not a little irritated—finally opening the door. If God decided to grant your request, according to Jesus, it wouldn't be out of any fond feelings in that moment but rather in response to the shameless audacity of your having asked.

Most of us were born with just this sort of audacity with respect to our earthly parents. Without the least embarrassment and without the slightest interest in the financial impossibility or the wantonness of our desires, we demanded pricey toys we saw on television, the brand name clothes our friends were wearing, and permission to participate in activities we knew were not in our best interest. From babyhood, my daughters demanded all kinds of miracles of me. "Fix it!" they cried, when some plaything they loved was impossibly broken. "It's *not* too late!" they insisted, when we arrived behind schedule or ran out of time for some planned amusement. For them, it was easy to demand things. They believed I had magical powers to produce whatever made them happy and to restore whatever went awry. They also understood that they were loved.

In the churches I have attended since returning to faith, I am often told that miracles no longer happen—a view that derives from the popular doctrine of dispensationalism, the theory that God interacts with people differently in different historical periods. Miracles were necessary in biblical times, dispensationalists say, to establish the authority of those who wrote scripture and started the church, but they are no longer necessary—and thus no longer happen—in the current dispensation. As a consequence of such faith-squelching teaching, believers often limit their prayers to what they think God wants for them, not what they want for themselves. When student athletes at my university pray aloud about upcoming games, for instance, they never pray to win, but only that no one will get hurt.

Believers weighed down by terrible suffering characteristically squeeze every drop of shamelessness and audacity out of their prayers. In praying for the terminally ill, they take a wide detour around their real desire for healing and restoration and offer up, instead, a wan petition for God's speed or reduced pain or peace for the family members. Instead of daring to pray for life, they race pell-mell in the opposite direction, straight ahead into the death they long not just to forestall or sweeten but to eliminate entirely.

I'm not saying that a bold prayer will necessarily be answered with a miracle, but only that miracles may be, even today, a key way God interacts with us. To our own disadvantage, though, we don't dare to ask for miracles. And, when we *do* ask—or when we have asked unawares, in groaning entreaties that underlie our holier requests that God's will be done—we often don't notice or rationalize away or even actively deny that the miracle we asked for has actually happened. We thus routinely discount and reject the possibility that God really does want to give us good things—not just the good things God knows we need but the same sort of crazy, pointless, impossible treats with which we lesser parents, if we had God's power, might set out to delight our own children.

Once, when my daughters were just little, our beagle had a large litter of puppies. While my husband was checking on them just before bedtime, one of the little pups got caught in the swinging barn door and broke its leg. It was not yet weaned and thus unlikely to be able to wear a cast successfully enough to compete for a teat, so my husband came back to the house and told us the poor little yelping creature would have to be euthanized. Charlotte and Lulu, appalled, insisted that we take the pup immediately to the vet, ignoring our objections that it was already past their bedtime and the vet would have to make an expensive after-hours trip up to the clinic to meet us. After a vain attempt to talk them out of their naive hope that anything could be done for the puppy even with medical assistance, we reluctantly agreed to their demand.

While Kris went back to the barn to get the puppy, the girls sat on the stairs in their PJs and prayed, passionately, that God would heal the little pup. I almost stopped them, I'm embarrassed to admit, because I didn't want them to be disappointed. And when Kris returned with the puppy, whimpering and huge-eyed in a shoebox with its little leg bent pitifully in two, it was all I could do not to talk the girls out of their silly anticipation of its recovery. When we got to the clinic, though, the vet stood the puppy up on the slippery examination table, felt along its legs, and pronounced that there was absolutely nothing wrong with it. The girls shouted, "Answered prayer! Answered prayer!"

I wish I could end this story with that happy ending, the resurrection of a puppy we weren't even planning to keep and the fulfillment of my daughters' impossible wish—certain proofs that God is as crazy in love with my girls as I am. I would like to argue that all we have to do is this simple thing of believing, with the confidence of children, in a God who longs to give us good things and we will be astonished with the health and happiness, the unlikely news of great joy, that will result. Alas, the faith of a child is hard to get to, and hard to maintain. As we mature, skepticism and practicality—and learned resignation to a world in which miracles never happen—get in the way. So, even Charlotte, though only five or six at the time, exhibited small signs of these impediments to faith not long after witnessing this miracle in answer to her prayer. A year or two later, when the story of the little pup came up at dinner, she announced that the miraculous healing had never happened. She had come up with a much more sensible analysis: "We only *thought* its leg was broken," she explained, and she has held to that view ever since.

Thinking back over the episode—as I have many times since it happened, recognizing in my daughter's response my own meager faith—I am struck anew by the wretchedness of our lot. We desire God's attendance in our lives, but then, when we are granted clear evidence that God *is* present and paying attention and even enjoying being with us, we reject the notion as illogical or coincidental, and thus impossible. I have no trouble imagining what God—still in those rumpled pajamas but now wide awake and a little out of breath—looks like upon returning to the door with the bread we wanted and finding that we have already turned away in despair.

God probably won't answer every bold prayer as dramatically as my daughters' plea was answered. And some prayers, it seems to me, would be like my own daughters' frequent demands for unwholesome objects and freedoms, demands to which even I, in my besottedness, automatically say no. The story of the prodigal son notwithstanding, it's hard for me to believe God would supply material wealth or earthly success in response to prayer. Also, even when God does respond to prayers by providing miracles, they may not be the miracles you envision. You may get a medical intervention that effects a temporary respite, rather than a total and spontaneous restoration to health. Or contentment, when you asked for an escape from your present circumstances. Or a delicious offer of forgiveness from a loved one, when you asked for time to reverse itself and let you undo a meanness. These, too, are miracles and worthy of celebration. And it may be God doesn't grant your wish at all. Doing so is, of course, *God's* choice, not yours. But you will never know unless you allow yourself to batter God's door with shameless audacity.

Just consider the things people in scripture have prayed for—and received! The Israelites, starving in the desert, prayed for bread, and God rained down manna. Solomon prayed for wisdom and got it. Jabez prayed, "enlarge my territory" and "keep me from harm so that I will be free from pain," and, we're told, "God granted his request" (I Chronicles 4:10). On his deathbed, Hezekiah prayed not to die, and God added fifteen years to his life. Hezekiah also prayed that, as a sign, the shadow on the stairway of Ahaz would move backward ten steps—in other words, that the progress of the sun in the sky would reverse itself—and it did. In a similar story, worried that the sun would set before one of his battles was done, Joshua prayed for God to stop time altogether, and "The sun stopped in the middle of the sky and delayed going down about a full day" (Joshua 10:13).

Often, in a spasm of stress to finish some pressing work, I, too, have prayed for God to slow time, and, although the writer of the book of Joshua says of Joshua's miraculous time-stopping that "There has never been a day like it before or since" (Joshua 10:14), I have found myself not only miraculously able to get everything done but aware of God's attendance as I worked.

Once, I made a bargain to read scripture every day, if God would just create space of time each day in which I could do it. Bargaining with God is another shamelessly audacious way of praying that many pastors and theologians object to, but I was desperate. A brand-new believer at the time, I was impatient to be someone who pursued God's will eagerly. I wanted to quit sinning and not have to force myself to do good, and I was hugely disappointed that becoming a Christian didn't automatically cause me to abandon my ingrained meanness and enable me to love others as effortlessly as I love myself. Why didn't I turn nice, I wondered, as most of the Christians I knew seemed to be: patient with my husband and daughters; affectionate and sweet-spirited toward my mother-in-law; uplifting toward and uncritical of my students and co-workers, no matter how difficult some of them were? I worked at these goals constantly but invariably failed even so.

I was especially frustrated when I came across Paul's comment on the efficacy of scripture toward these ends. "All Scripture is God-breathed and is useful for teaching, rebuking, correcting and training in righteousness," Paul counseled his younger fellow believer Timothy, "so that all God's people may be thoroughly equipped for every good work" (2 Timothy 3:16–17). I longed to breathe in the divine breath of scripture and thus equip myself to do good works. But, with two toddling daughters and a full-time job at our local school, the only time I had for reading were the couple of hours at morning before the girls got up, and, with six writing classes, I had to spend that time grading papers. So, I came up with a deal: If God would see to it that I got my grading done, I would join my husband in reading the Bible every morning at breakfast.

My bargain was a smaller act of faith than it may sound. I offered it somewhat sardonically, not really expecting anything to change. And nothing did, exactly. I stayed just as busy at work. As I always had, I graded a few papers here and there throughout the day—in class while my students wrote, between answering questions and conducting emergency peer editing sessions and disciplining misbehavior; on duty out in the parking lot during lunch; surreptitiously on a clipboard at pep assemblies; and in the school library during my scanty free time. I couldn't tell that I got more papers graded that way than I ever had. Nevertheless, somehow, miraculously, I was able to get it all done, and, at morning, I opened the Bible and breathed and read. I never took another paper home that whole year.

Perhaps it was the spiritual focus of my bargain prayer that made it so successful. I wanted to read scripture—surely a worthy goal—and God empowered me to do so. Jesus specifically promises that God answers prayers for the Holy Spirit—literally, for God's holy breath, not only the source of scripture and human life but of all spiritual gifts—just as readily as human fathers give their children the good things they ask for. "If you then, though you are evil, know how to give good gifts to your children," he told his disciples, "how much more will your Father in heaven give the Holy Spirit to those who ask him!" (Luke 11:13). God was eager to give me the gift of the Holy Spirit—that is, to empower me to do the good thing I wanted to do. All I had to do was have the shameless audacity to ask.

Like Charlotte with the beagle pup, though, I later discredited this miraculous gift of time by counseling fellow teachers, at writing pedagogy workshops I led in the years that followed, to simply decide not to bring work home and it would somehow get done. I relegated the miracle, in other words, to the realm of human will or positive thinking or the principle that work expands—or shrinks—to fill the time allotted for it. I saw what God had given me as the product of *my* will, *my* positive thinking, *my* work. Having repackaged God's lovely gift in this way, I ended up losing it and resuming my old breakfast table habits after that glorious year of breathing God's breath daily.

People don't really look at spiritual gifts the same way they do other gifts, it seems to me. As presents, that is. Delightful surprises, often arriving, like Christmas gifts, after an exciting period of waiting and expectation. It may be a matter of semantics in the original Greek that I don't have the skills to sort out. According to my exhaustive concordance, when Jesus spoke of "gifts"—the good "gifts" fathers give their children (Matthew 7:11, Luke 11:13), the "gift" Jews offered to God at the altar (Matthew 5:23), and the "gift of

God" that is himself (John 4:10)—he used the words δῶμα (*dōma*), δῶρον (*dōron*), and δωρεά (*dōrea*), all three derived from the Greek word δίδωμι (*didōmi*), which means *to give*. When Paul wrote of the "gifts" of prophecy, tongues, healing, and miraculous powers and counseled believers to "eagerly desire spiritual gifts" (I Corinthians 14:1), he used the completely different and much more spiritually loaded word χάρισμα (*charisma*), derived from the Greek word for *grace*. Even so, since the two words are routinely translated identically in English versions of the Bible, they are interchangeable for the English-speaking readers, and the way believers typically talk about "spiritual gifts" tends to focus on the spiritual-ness of the gifts in question to the exclusion of their "gift-ness."

Consequently, when I was a new believer, as ardently as I longed for spiritual gifts—and as disappointed as I also was that I didn't automatically grow such spiritual fruits as patience, mercy, niceness, and liking to be around sick people—I nevertheless saw such gifts and fruits as things I had to somehow make happen. They were not gifts, really. Not eagerly awaited presents from God. Not even—like fruits—the natural products of a faith that swelled in me and emerged, almost entirely independent of any intentional input of my own. Certainly they were not delightful surprises, like the gigantic zucchinis that appear like miracles in my garden. Rather, they were behaviors that, as a believer, I needed to somehow *do*. And, regrettably, I didn't do them.

I think this misperception of spiritual gifts and fruits as laudable Christian behaviors, rather than as the miraculous empowerments they actually are, is what keeps us from shamelessly and audaciously desiring them. We may speak of grace as a "gift" freely given, but we don't actually believe that God, having long since given up on the hope that we will do good on our own, magically equips us with the Holy Spirit. We don't think of the gifts and fruits of the Spirit as amazing feats of God, available to believers for the asking.

Never was the miraculous nature of spiritual gifts made as clear to me as when I once, contrary to my own inclination and talents and desires, contrary to the very essence of my personality, tended to some elderly neighbors in a health emergency. June and Claris were sisters, both retired teachers and widowed, who shared a well groomed ranch house near our farm. I had become acquainted with them early in my marriage when some heifers of ours got spooked, broke through a fence, and ended up in their yard. Several deliveries of home-baked bread later—offered in atonement for their trampled pansies—I served with them on a children's ministry committee at our church.

I didn't like them very much. They were given to sanctimonious diatribes on the rottenness of "kids these days"—and, as a mom of a kid in Claris's Sunday school class, I knew these included mine— and endless reveries on how perfect their own, now remote children had been by comparison. At the committee meeting, whenever anyone suggested anything, the two of them smiled politely at each other and went pointedly silent, making clear to the rest of us that they knew in advance that whatever it was would fail. Worst of all—from the perspective of someone still suffering from trauma caused by a gun to her head—I once encountered a nephew of theirs hunting, without permission, on our land. When I asked him who he was and what he thought he was doing there—using a rifle, in easy range of our daughters, cattle, and dogs—he said they'd told him we wouldn't mind.

Nevertheless, June and Claris seemed to like me and occasionally showed up at my door with foraged delicacies they knew I'd appreciate: morel mushrooms, hickory nuts, catfish the nephew had caught, and, once, a brace of pheasants, already cleaned and skinned but with their stunning red-plumed heads still intact for identification. So, when I heard that Claris had cancer, I felt bad for her and went to their house to see if I could be of service.

Things were worse than I expected. June came to the door and peered at me a few seconds as though she didn't know me, then let me in without saying anything and remained standing by the door, as if expecting to let me back out again any second. It was a pleasantly cool and fresh fall day out, but inside the house it was stifling hot and dusty and reeked of a refrigerator that needed to be cleaned.

In the short time since I had last seen either of them—it couldn't have been more than a few months—they'd gotten inexplicably ancient and decrepit looking. Claris slumped in an armchair in front of the TV. She offered me coffee and cookies, looking over at June and fumbling for an aluminum cane at her feet. I quickly declined— as much to save Claris the trouble as to avoid having to eat anything in that smelly house—but she seemed so downcast that I changed my mind and offered to make some coffee for all of us. June sank into the armchair next to Claris without responding and stared expressionlessly at the TV.

I waded through a clump of Wal-Mart bags loaded with unopened packages of paper towels to the coffee machine, rummaged in the cupboards until Claris called from the other room that the coffee was in the refrigerator, started the coffee, and then washed some cups from the dirty dishes piled up in the sink. Their milk had gone bad, and the only sugar I could find was caked into a hard mass at the bottom of a sticky, rooster-shaped sugar bowl, but I found an open package of Oreos and arranged a few on a plate to look pretty. After I had served us, I forced myself to stay just long enough to get the news on how Claris was doing. They struggled to tell me, stumbling through unpronounceable words the doctor had given them and accounts of medicine prices and generic versus name brands and alternative treatments that they were sure would cure her but that weren't covered by her insurance. Claris nodded tiredly. *I couldn't wait to get out of there.*

Here are people in need, I rebuked myself as I drove the mile or so home. *Widows! Neighbors, if there ever were neighbors.* I had always been impressed with my husband's simpleminded conviction that loving one's neighbors meant precisely that: loving the ones who lived nearby us. *I should have washed their dishes. Offered to pick up.* I resolved to visit them regularly. Start bringing them food. Perhaps overcome my hypersensitivity to smells long enough to clean out that refrigerator. Still, it was months before I managed to make myself go there again, this time taking Kris with me.

Claris was in the back bedroom, June told us when she finally came to the door and let us in. She looked agitated. She said she would go get her sister, hesitated, then disappeared for a long time. Kris and I stood in the foyer, looking at each other. After a while, we went into the living room and pretended to watch TV. The house was an utter mess, every surface piled up with catalogs and old newspapers and fast food containers and mucky spoons—for medicine, I guessed—in plastic sandwich bags. I felt drugged by reluctance and regret. *Why did I come here?* I wailed inwardly. But, eventually, I managed to force myself into the kitchen. The floor space was almost completely taken up now with paper goods in Wal-Mart bags and the counter with medicine bottles, Pop-Tart and cookie boxes, and little plastic tubs of Jell-O in different colors. *That's what they're planning to eat for the next few weeks,* I speculated nervously. Before I could motivate myself to investigate further, much less take up any of the tasks I knew I should be doing, I heard noises from the back of the house somewhere, little cries from Claris and June saying something in response that sounded distressed, and I knew I had to go back there and see if I could help.

For many minutes I could not make myself do it. Everything in me resisted. Kris just stood there, in the living room where I had left him, looking horrified. I had to force myself down the hall leg by leg, like a child making a doll walk.

I found them in a dark, paneled bedroom barely lit by a pair of feeble sconce fixtures. Rubbery brown curtains were pulled tightly closed over the one window, and the bed was stacked with clothes on hangers. June was trying to help Claris to the adjoining bathroom, but Claris couldn't make it any farther. She was naked from the waist down.

"I can't! I can't!" she whimpered.

She hadn't had a bowel movement in two weeks, June told me grimly. We helped her over to a vinyl recliner, where June said her sister had been sleeping. The second we got her in the chair, her bowels released in a spectacular flood of diarrhea.

In that second, I became someone else. There's no other way to satisfactorily explain it. I am inexperienced in all matters related to health care. I'm also all but crippled, as I have said, by an overly sensitive sense of smell. I've always avoided hospitals for this reason, and I'm actively repulsed by sick people. Added to that, I'd never liked being around Claris in the first place, and the dreadful intimacy of seeing a woman whom I hardly knew and had no love for without her clothes on just about undid me. Somehow, though, I overcame all of these hindrances and took command. I sent June out to have Kris call an ambulance, then got washcloths and towels from a cupboard in the bathroom and cleaned Claris up as best I could, clucking and reassuring her all the while, as I do when one of my daughters throws up in the night. I covered her up with a dressing gown I found on the bed so she wouldn't be embarrassed when the paramedics got there, and, after they showed up and got her onto a stretcher and into the ambulance, I sent Kris and June after them in our car and stayed behind to clean up properly.

One might explain it by saying that the adrenaline of sheer horror kicked in and empowered me to do what had to be done. Or that, however disinclined, as a woman I was genetically wired to know what to do in a caregiving emergency as well as motivated to do it against my own inclination. But the aspect of this experience that I find most compelling, the part that evidences the miraculous action of the Holy Spirit in me and the unequivocal presence of God in that place, is that, from the moment I entered the dim back bedroom and throughout the hours I subsequently spent first washing and rinsing and drying that recliner, fold by fold, and mopping the floor and laundering the loads of towels and washcloths I used in the process and then going methodically through the house, room by room, clearing and sanitizing every surface, washing the dishes, cleaning out the refrigerator—during that whole time, I had no sense of smell. More than that, even: I had no aversion to any part of this work. I enjoyed it. I can explain it no other way than that it was a miracle.

In the months that followed my first visit to June and Claris, I had prayed mightily for release from myself—release from the judgmentalism that prevented me from liking them as well as my overweening reluctance to help someone I knew was in need—but it never occurred to me that I was asking for the biggest miracle of my life to date. And the miracle was not exactly what I had asked for. Not just the temporary release from myself and the ability, in this one instance, to do God's will effortlessly, although I did receive these amazing gifts as well. The real miracle—the gift, the fruit, the delight—was that the whole experience was pleasurable. Putting that house right. Getting things clean and sweet-smelling for when June came home. Gathering up all those sticky medicine spoons—there must have been forty or fifty of them—from every room of the house. Folding the clean towels and washcloths and stacking them neatly in the bathroom cupboard. It was the most enjoyable work I have ever done. It didn't even seem like work, really—unless, maybe, it was the thornless, painless, happy work assigned to the first humans: tilling the crumbly black soil of Eden, while the God of heaven and earth strolled along beside them, enjoying their company.

I ❧ Many believers limit their prayers to desires they think God wants for them, not what they want for themselves. Certainly there's nothing wrong with putting God's will before one's own in prayer, as in Jesus' own agonized prayer on the Mount of Olives, "not my will, but yours be done" (Luke 22:42), as well as in the model prayer he offers his disciples: "your will be done" (Matthew 6:10). By contrast, though, little children, whom Jesus recommends we emulate in faith, pray with no holds barred. My daughters, from babyhood, prayed about the most minute details of their lives—lost toys, being dumped by elementary school boyfriends, revenge on each other after a fight. Often, even when they prayed in anger or maliciousness, I sensed a peace in them after they prayed, as though God had heard and wasn't appalled to be invited into such absurdities and spite. It's never wrong to pray about anything. Never. You may not receive what you pray for, but you will enjoy God's presence in the least significant areas of your life—areas that, without God's presence, often accrue much larger significance than they should. Practice praying forbidden prayers. Pray for minor assistance, such as help in locating your misplaced car keys. Pray that the enraged driver who just zoomed dangerously past you will be pulled over and ticketed. Pray to ace a test. Pray to win.

2 ❧ Learn to pray with shameless audacity. Remember, praying is nothing more than communicating what's on your mind to a listening, caring God. God will not answer every bold prayer, but you will never know unless you pray it. Allow yourself to ask for impossible deliverance or help in some matter of importance to you.

3 ❧ Whenever you pray, be on the alert for and keep track of any apparent response. Paying attention to God's potential presence in response to a bold prayer is as important as allowing yourself to pray it in the first place. Remember that God may not answer every bold prayer dramatically, or as you expect, or at all. Remember, too, that praying is nothing more than communicating what's on your mind to a listening, caring God.

4 ❧ Think of a person who loves you. How do you know that person loves you? How does that person typically show his or her love? What gifts—tangible and intangible—have you received from that person? How would that person feel if you returned a gift from him or her unopened? Now think about God in these terms.

CHAPTER THIRTEEN

God with Us—Visibly, Audibly, Tangibly

IT'S A BIT LATE in a book written by a Christian on the subject of the divine presence to start talking about Jesus Christ as the seeable, hearable, touchable manifestation of an otherwise *unseeable*, *unhearable*, *untouchable* God. The apostle Paul—who never met Christ in the flesh—refers to him as "the image of the invisible God" (Colossians 1:15) and argues that our alienation from God is repaired by "Christ's physical body through death" (Colossians 1:22). Paul is referring, of course, to Jesus' sacrificial death for our sins, through which we are reunited with God, but the incarnation of Jesus—that is, the fact that he became one of us—repairs our alienation from God in another way. As a human being, Jesus was fully present: as seeable and hearable and touchable as any other person we might meet. Jesus *was*, in other words, the "physical presence" of God, hence the name by which Isaiah heralded Jesus' coming: Immanuel, which means, God *With* Us.

The gospel writers, at least a couple of whom scholars believe knew Jesus personally or had seen him with his own eyes, focus again and again on the physicality of his interaction with the people around him. They show him shouting across a lake, calling fishermen to come follow him. They show him spitting in the dirt to make mud and smearing it in the eyes of a blind man to restore his sight. They show him squatting to scratch words in the dust. They show him being anointed by weeping women, his feet washed with their tears and dried with their hair. They show Jesus weeping himself on several occasions. They show him stripped, lashed, spat on. They show his brutalized body nailed onto wood beams and raised up, naked, for all to see. In their accounts of Jesus' appearances after his death and resurrection—when even his closest friends, in astonishment and disbelief, struggled to recognize him—the gospel writers take pains to show that, even then, having survived death, Jesus was still indisputably human and real and not a ghost. Jesus asked for some of the grilled fish his friends were eating. He cooked breakfast for them on the beach. He thrust his hands out before the doubting among them to expose the holes where the nails had been and parted his robe to show the place on his side where the sword had entered and blood and water had run out of him, proving that he had actually died.

The problem with God With Us as concrete evidence of God's invisible presence is that, having risen from death and ascended back to heaven, Jesus is once again invisible. His physical reality amounts to, for modern Bible readers, words on a page, written by people whose identities scholars dispute and who were writing long after the events they recorded.

And, although the gospel writers did emphasize Jesus' physical presence in the stories they told of his life, they routinely omitted certain physical details that might have helped us to see and hear and touch Jesus in our minds today. We don't know, for instance, what Jesus looked like, what color his hair was, whether he wore it long or short. Although he typically wears a beard in the pictures made of him in the centuries after his death, we don't know for sure if he was actually bearded or clean shaven. It is nowhere recorded whether he was spare or more fleshy or if his voice was rough or smooth, loud or soft. We don't know if his embrace was hard and quick or warm and sensual. And there is not one reference, in all the gospels, to Jesus laughing or even smiling.

Although we have dependable physical representations and artifacts of others who have gone before us—Abraham Lincoln, for example, or Moctezuma of Tenochtitlan—we have no dependable physical evidence of Jesus' life on earth. No photographs or even contemporaneous paintings or sculptures that record what he looked like. No death mask. No bones or snippets of hair. Not even a tomb we can point to and say, unequivocally, "Here is where, for a few days, his dead body lay." As prone as we are to depend on the evidence of past existence in our grieving and archiving of past heroes and even villains, it seems a miracle that no such proofs have been passed down through the centuries and that every attempt to argue that one such relic is really real has been rendered silly by scientists and logicians. It seems, in other words, that God must have planned it to be thus. That God wanted our faith to seek other substantiation that God was—and is—*with* us than a presence we could see and hear and touch.

Jesus said as much himself. He commended modern believers, long in advance of their time, for their ability to have faith in him *without* any physical evidence of him and belittled the faith of his own disciples, who had been given the "knowledge of the secrets of the kingdom of heaven" (Matthew 13:11)—who had not only seen Jesus but witnessed his amazing miracles with their own eyes, who had heard Jesus' voice speaking to them unambiguously, who had embraced Jesus in greeting and eaten meals with him and touched their lips to his cheek—but who nevertheless didn't understand what he was trying to tell them.

"Truly I tell you," Jesus lamented, "many prophets and righteous people longed to see what you see but did not see it, and to hear what you hear but did not hear it" (Matthew 13:17). And, chiding his dinner companions for complaining that the money a woman had spent on perfume for anointing him could have been spent on the poor, he said, "The poor you will always have with you, but you will not always have me" (Matthew 26:11). The God who sent us God With Us also took him away from us, at least for the time being.

Where does that leave us, as believers? Christians often speak of Jesus in vibrant, present, real-sounding terms. We sing songs about seeing Jesus' face and holding him. Even in the absence of details about his physical appearance, we make pictures of what he might have looked like, pictures that often say more about us than about someone of his time and place, racial heritage, and social standing. In popular art, we depict Jesus reaching out to us, embracing us, carrying us in his arms. The sad reality, though, is that even God With Us, the physical manifestation of God on Earth, must be experienced vicariously these days.

Before exploring what this vicarious experience of an absent Jesus might be like, it's useful to consider some of our secondhand experiences of God in general. As beings created "in the image of God" (Genesis 1:27), we share key traits and habits and attitudes of God. Like God—and unlike other creatures not made in God's image—we make things and work and rest from our work. We value companionship, we're jealous of others' love and attention, and we suffer pain when those we love turn away from us.

Almost every relational role we play with others expresses God's relationship with us, in some way. As a parent, for example, I vicariously coexperience God's parenting of humankind. Charlotte and Lulu are frequently disobedient and self-centered and mean-spirited, just as were the humans God created and nurtured and cherished. Thus, through my interactions with my daughters, I sense a little of the intense pain God must feel when we humans turn away to pursue desires that cannot be good for us. As a parent, I know, too, why God so values our repentance and gratitude. No achievement of Charlotte or Lulu thrills me like their very occasional expressions of remorse for some offense or thanks for some act of love or mercy on my behalf. By thinking about God as a fellow parent, in other words, I can coexperience God's sufferings on my own behalf. I can also get a sense of God's occasional joy when I'm affectionate in return or make even a failed attempt to do the right thing.

A friend once disapproved of my anthropomorphizing God in this way, saying that doing so cheapened God's supremacy and power. To my mind, though, the fact that we were made in God's image legitimizes such speculations and comparisons—although there is always the danger that we will begin to envision a God created in *our* image, rather than the reverse. With that warning in mind, return with me to Jesus, "the image of the invisible God" (Colossians 1:15).

Because Jesus was God in human form, we share even more of his traits and habits, feelings and attitudes. We have the same kind of body as he had. The same sensory experience of the world. The same needs. We hunger for the same food—physical and spiritual—as Jesus did during his forty-day fast in the desert. Like him, we make friends and enemies. We crave love and respect. We mourn when those we love get sick or die. We suffer. Isaiah describes God With Us as "despised and rejected by others/a man of suffering, and familiar with pain" (Isaiah 53:3), and most of us have had or will have experiences of sorrow, pain, or distress in our lives. Many have been falsely accused at one time or another. Some of us have suffered meanness and violence at others' hands. Like Jesus, we often long, in vain, for others to understand what we know to be true. These shared experiences of misery link us to Jesus and bring him close. Almost near enough to touch.

Jesus may also be experienced vicariously through his sonship. Jesus himself invites us to experience him this way when he tells us that we, too, are God's children, his siblings. As God's son—and in many ways a distinct being from God the Father, although both are God—Jesus has the same kind of relationship with God that we also enjoy with God, a relationship that mirrors, in effect, the relationship we may have with our earthly parents. Like us with our own parents as well as with our divine Parent, Jesus counts on God's protection and love, yet struggles to obey a parent whose will is sometimes at odds with his own. He values God's advice. God's praise is his most precious reward, God's disapproval the most feared punishment. Thus, Jesus' experiences as God's son can resonate with our own relationships as sons and daughters with our earthly parents and with God, thereby giving experiential substance to both Jesus' and his Father's presence.

As fellow children of God, we might also get a sense of Jesus' presence by thinking of Jesus as a genuine sibling. It's kind of tricky for me to imagine Jesus as my actual brother—as a peer in the most essential sense, vying, as siblings typically do, for the attention and approval of a shared parent. My own daughters, even at fifteen and sixteen, still fight over which one gets to sit on my lap when they're feeling affectionate. Often one of them will sneak up when the other's not looking and beg to be loved best. According to our human child-rearing standards, good parents love all their children the same, but

God the Father surely loves Jesus best. I'm guessing, if I really considered myself to be Jesus' sister, that God's preference for my brother over me would rankle as much as it did for my siblings and me when our father—in jest, he insists—referred to the older of our two brothers as his "Number One Son." Imagine being there with Jesus, along with his cousin John the Baptist (who devoted himself to God to the extreme of subsisting on bugs), when God declared from heaven, "This is my Son, whom I love; with him I am well pleased" (Matthew 3:17). If I had been there when God spoke those words and if Jesus had been my actual brother—or cousin or colleague or fellow rabbi—I'm sure I would have felt slighted. Nevertheless, thinking about Jesus as an actual sibling, even as the enviably perfect and favored son of a biased father, brings him down from the ether of abstract ideas into which I tend to relegate him and thereby enhances my sense of his realness and presence.

Generally speaking, the "presence" of someone or something is perceived as an otherness: I see or hear or smell or taste or touch something that is *not* me and thus sense its presence. In American Sign Language, *presence* is indicated by bringing one's hands up and almost together, as though about to clap, representing two people coming face to face with each other. Curiously, though, Jesus describes his presence for believers as an indwelling: "I am the vine; you are the branches. If you remain in me and I in you, you will bear much fruit; apart from me you can do nothing" (John 15:5). Paul complicates this metaphor by casting the whole church—that is, all who believe in Jesus as God's son sent to save them—as Jesus' "body": "Now you are the body of Christ, and each one of you is a part of it" (I Corinthians 12:27). Jesus and the believer—or, in Paul's analogy, Jesus and all believers—are, in other words, part of the same entity.

Sensing the presence of a person who is part of you—and you

of him—is problematic. Just trying to explain such a concept, as Paul does to the Corinthians, can end up sounding comic:

> Now if the foot should say, "Because I am not a hand, I do not belong to the body," it would not for that reason cease to be part of the body. And if the ear should say, "Because I am not an eye, I do not belong to the body," it would not for that reason cease to be part of the body. If the whole body were an eye, where would the sense of hearing be? If the whole body were an ear, where would the sense of smell be? . . . .
>
> The eye cannot say to the hand, "I don't need you!" And the head cannot say to the feet, "I don't need you!" On the contrary, those parts of the body that seem to be weaker are indispensable, and the parts that we think are less honorable we treat with special honor. (I Corinthians 12:15–17, 21–23)

If Jesus is within us, and we in him, then sensing his presence amounts to, in some sense, being aware of ourselves.

One aspect of ourselves that clearly evidences the presence of the divine is, as Jesus suggests, the fruit of our shared vine. We sense Jesus' presence, in other words, when we are conscious of *being* Jesus—as I was when I cleaned up after Claris' accident. Jesus wasn't just *with* me in that situation; he *was* me. His power and love replaced, temporarily, all my reluctance and resistance and meanness. It was not my hands that dipped washcloths in soapy water and scrubbed that recliner, not my nose that sucked in the foul air of that room and perceived it as odorless. It was Jesus, in me, or me in him, who did that sweet work of kindness. I sensed his presence not only in my sudden, miraculous ability to put others' comforts before my own but in my utterly uncharacteristic joy in doing so.

Sensing Jesus' wonderful presence in us thus involves first desiring spiritual fruit, then pursuing it despite our inevitable unwillingness, and finally, and most important, paying attention when we receive it. In my case, I experienced Jesus' presence in me as a sudden enjoyment of what would have been an onerous and offensive task. A release from who I was and an instantaneous transformation into a perfect, loving, selfless version of me—namely, into Jesus himself.

Jesus also invites us to experience his presence in others, specifically those who are—or should be—the recipients of our acts of generosity and compassion. In the last of a string of stories in Matthew's gospel that Jesus offers in response to his disciples' questions about what to expect at "the end of the age" (Matthew 24:3), the Son of Man—the name Jesus routinely uses for himself—sits on his heavenly throne, surrounded by angels, and divides the nations into two groups. He rewards the first group for showing him hospitality when he was hungry and thirsty and friendless, clothing him when he was naked, caring for him when he was sick, and visiting him in prison. The second group is punished with eternal damnation for not doing any of these acts of compassion. Neither group—again, it would be comic, but for the seriousness of this story—remembers ever having encountered the Son of Man in such circumstances, and to each group Jesus identifies himself as the human recipients of their kindness.

"Truly I tell you," he says to the first group, "whatever you did for one of the least of these brothers and sisters of mine, you did for me" (Matthew 25:40). And to the second group he says, "Truly I tell you, whatever you did not do for one of the least of these, you did not do for me" (Matthew 25:45). The Son of Man is, in this story, quite literally present, both to the saved and the damned, in the guise of needy human beings.

At a church I used to attend, I had an intense sense of Jesus' presence in a semihomeless person the congregation on and off supported—an older woman with mental health problems who wore her long white hair loose like a young girl's. She shuffled rather than walked, laughed inappropriately—sometimes during the worship service—and often spoke with jarring candor about matters not generally talked about in public. If she had a cold and her nose ran, she just let it.

When I met Louanne outside of church, she had typically just emerged from some grim catastrophe and regaled me with an account so detailed and relentlessly sequential that it always made me late for wherever I was going. Her apartment caught fire—not once, but three separate times. She was mistaken for someone else—amazingly, since she was so unusual looking—and arrested. She lost the boot-shaped car in which she mostly lived in a vast mall parking lot and had to sleep in a restroom cubicle and beg for food for days before a security guard was able to help her find the car again, parked right where she had left it.

If I had any money, I felt obliged to give it to her—Louanne surely needed it way more than I did, I reasoned—and I came to dread running into her anywhere but in the safe pews and fellowship hall of our church, where there were other people for her to latch on to and parenting duties to escape to and a reliable order of events that structured our interaction.

Wherever I encountered Louanne, though, I had an overwhelming sense of the presence of Jesus. There is no other way to describe it. In the midst of one of her stories, I'd be willing myself not to look at my watch and suddenly think, just as Jacob did upon waking from his dream in the desert, "Surely the LORD is in this place, and I was not aware of it" (Genesis 28:16). When Louanne squeezed past my family at the start of the service, I felt sudden awe, as though Jesus himself had touched me, and one of Louanne's guffaws, exploding an unexceptional sermon or prayer into strange fragments of embarrassment for all present, was, for me, the laughter of Jesus never written of in the gospels.

One Sunday, I had a sense of this woman as Jesus simultaneously with a sense of *myself* as Jesus interacting with her. This is complicated, I know—kind of like looking at the night sky and realizing that you are seeing an infinity of stars, all so far away as to have existed centuries before you were born—but let me try to tell it anyway. It was at church. Charlotte was just little at the time and had insisted on wearing a pair of gigantic, bright blue satin platform shoes—styled like athletic shoes—that she had made me pay three dollars for at the Salvation Army. The shoes were hideous, especially in combination with her delicate church dress and bow-shaped barrettes. They were also too big for her and so ridiculously tall that she could barely walk in them. But Charlotte, who has always had a thing for odd shoes, was very proud of them. So, in the interest of communicating that church was a place where one got to wear special clothes in honor of God, I had let her wear them.

Between Sunday school and the actual service, there was a fellowship time, with cookies, coffee, and packets of cocoa and cider to mix with hot water. Charlotte had recently discovered the thrill of mixing two packets of cocoa into one Styrofoam cup of hot water to make the lukewarm sludge that was the best part of church for most of the kids there. They liked the process of making this drink as much as the drink itself, I think, and they got the powder and that sludge all over the place, causing several churchgoers to object. It occurred to me that Charlotte's precarious shoes might result in her making an even bigger mess than usual, so I got in line with the kids so that I could at least oversee her part in the mess-making, even if she wouldn't let me help her.

Louanne got in line behind us. It wasn't long before she spotted Charlotte's shoes and remarked upon them, bellowing in her over-loud voice, "Those have got to be the *uuugggliest* shoes I have ever seen in my life!"

Everyone in the fellowship hall looked down at the shoes. Charlotte looked down, too, and then up at Louanne, and I could see her little lip curve the way it always did when she was about to cry.

If you are a parent, you know the chaos of feelings that rose in me: defensiveness, mortification, rage. Everything in me lurched into position to protect my daughter from attack, and I was ready simultaneously to return the aggression and muffle the whole exchange to protect Charlotte from further embarrassment. At that moment, though, there flashed before me all the rash comments I had ever made in my life. There were many. I am the sort of person who speaks before thinking and speaks a lot. In that instant, I recognized myself in Louanne. Indeed, I *was* Louanne, in my mind—just as fecklessly inappropriate, just as messed up, and, somehow, just as mysteriously Jesus himself.

The confrontation dissolved finally in what I see now as a sluice of grace. I murmured some diffusing words about taste and the Salvation Army in Louanne's direction, Louanne was simultaneously distracted by some other offense ahead of us in the line, and Charlotte returned, with the preoccupation of a six-year-old with what's impor-tant, to her cocoa slush.

God With Us was only actually *with* humankind in the flesh for thirty-three years. Nevertheless, his presence outlives his bodily existence through the accounts of scripture, through our shared experience as fellow humans made in God's image, through his indwelling of believers, and through his representation in all who are in need. In the poor. The sick. The imprisoned. In all who suffer in this broken world. In you. In me. In us. With us.

I ⚶ People who are disabled report that others ignore or avoid looking at or simply don't see them. Those who are overweight often feel as though they are invisible to those around them. Similarly, the recently bereaved say that, after the initial flood of people offering condolence and help and attention, everyone deserts them and they feel more alone and miserable than ever. Actively seek Jesus' presence by being on the alert for people who feel unseen or abandoned by others. Notice them. Meet their eyes. Smile at them. Chat. Strive to enter their lives. Remind yourself, as you interact with those who suffer, that Jesus equated such sufferers with himself.

2 ⚶ Be Jesus to someone of your acquaintance in need of a companion—your mother-in-law, an elderly neighbor, a co-worker expected to retire any day, the friendless kid next door—by going out of your way to be present to him or her on a regular basis. What you do does not have to be anything big. If the person lives alone, you might simply call on occasion or invite yourself for a cup of coffee. If the person is unliked and avoided by others, you might go out of your way to say hello or to sit by him or her at lunch. You might chat with a young person at some public event.

3 ❧ Imagine what it would be like if Jesus were your actual brother. Be as specific as you can in imagining him as a part of your existing family. Where would he fall in the birth order of you and your siblings? Do you envision him younger than you or older? How would you likely interact? What confidences or activities would you share with him that you would share with no one besides a sibling? What would he know about you that only a sibling would know?

CHAPTER FOURTEEN

My God, My God, Why Have You Forsaken Me?

FEW HAVE SOUGHT God's presence so famously among the poor, sick, and hungry as Mother Teresa, whose fifty-year ministry began with a small convent in the slums of Calcutta and exploded into orphanages, schools, hospitals, homes for the dying, and soup kitchens all over the world. She devoted her life to those she referred to as the world's "unwanted" in the "dark holes" in which they lived[1]—dark not merely because of their misery and want but, more important for her, because God's light was absent from their lives. Paradoxically, it was Teresa's own yearning for God's luminous presence that took her into their darkness, but she didn't find any contradiction in this undertaking.

Our human longing for God, as Teresa saw it, is matched by God's longing for us, for, as she explained in a letter to a friend, "He too was hungry for love. So He made Himself the Hungry One, the Thirsty One, the Naked One, the Homeless [One] and kept on calling—I was hungry, naked, homeless." Taking Jesus at his word when he told the saved, "Truly I tell you, whatever you did for one of the least of these brothers and sisters of mine, you did for me"

(Matthew 25:40), Teresa responded to his call to "*Come, be My light*" to the needy not merely out of the desire to serve but because she expected to find Jesus himself in their darkness.

Thus the world's astonishment when, ten years after Mother Teresa's death, it became known that, throughout the entirety of her ministry, she had no sense of God's presence whatsoever. Far from the heightened awareness of God we might have supposed her to have experienced, far from an enhanced perception of God's attendance in her daily activities, Mother Teresa felt utterly abandoned and unwanted by God. For fifty years—a period beginning, as she says, "more or less from the time I started 'the work,'" and continuing, with one brief respite, until her death at the age of eighty-seven—she endured what she described as "this terrible sense of loss—this untold darkness—this loneliness, this continual longing for God— which gives me that pain deep down in my heart." She revealed what she called her "deepest secret" in anguished pleas for help scrawled to various spiritual advisers during those fifty years, letters in which she referred to God as "the Absent One" and characterized her life as an agony of spiritual loneliness: "Such deep longing for God—so deep that it is painful—a suffering continual—and yet not wanted by God—repulsed—empty—no faith—no love—no zeal.—Souls hold no attraction—Heaven means nothing—to me it looks like an empty place—the thought of it means nothing to me and yet this tortured longing for God." She was hyperaware of the contradiction of her situation and worried that others mistakenly thought that "faith, trust and love are filling my very being and that the intimacy with God and union to His will must be absorbing my heart.—Could they but know—and how my cheerfulness is the cloak by which I cover the emptiness and misery."

Despite Mother Teresa's lifelong efforts to hide her secret from the world, her private writings were published in a book focusing on her spiritual darkness, titled, with some irony, *Come Be My Light: The Private Writings of the "Saint of Calcutta."* Thus, a distressing detail of Mother Teresa's—and many others'—faith experience was presented for public consideration: that God may seem utterly absent even for long periods of a believer's spiritual journey.

By the time the world was finding out about Teresa's darkness, she had already been "beatified," step one in the often centuries long process of becoming an officially recognized Catholic saint. Strangely—at least to those of us not versed in Catholic saint lore— Teresa's experience of God's absence bolstered, rather than detracted from, her consideration for sainthood. Among saints, there is a long history of what Renaissance mystic St. John of the Cross referred to as the "dark night of the soul"[2]: a devout believer's inability to sense God's presence for a period of time characterized by excruciating emptiness, spiritual "darkness" or "dryness," fear, desolation, loneliness, and despair.

Dark night sufferers typically can't pray—or else their prayers feel empty and unheard. Not surprisingly, they struggle with doubt. Mother Teresa repeatedly questioned her faith. "They say people in hell suffer eternal pain because of the loss of God . . . In my soul I feel just that terrible pain of loss—of God not wanting me—of God not being God—of God not really existing," she agonized in a letter addressed to Jesus himself. More than once, she confessed, dully, "I have no faith—I don't believe." Paradoxically, she cited faith as her only support in her suffering: "within me everything is icy cold. It is only that blind faith that carries me through for in reality to me all is darkness."

Loneliness. Darkness. Blind faith. The potential condition of us all in believing in a God that can't be seen or heard or touched.

Reading snippets of Teresa's revelations in reviews of *Come Be My Light*, I was reminded of my long years of atheism, in which I felt first abandoned by God, then unsure of God's existence, and eventually, as Mother Teresa described, absolutely alone in a torment of longing.

When my husband was in college, there was a philosophy professor who had once been a preacher and often wrote editorials in the university newspaper. A story went around that once, while the man was waiting to be seated in a restaurant, a waitress asked him, "Are you alone?" When he answered yes, he realized that he really was. Entirely. Irrevocably. From that moment, it was said, he realized he was an atheist.

The main characteristic that distinguishes nonbelievers from saintly dark night sufferers—in the eyes of the Catholic Church, at least—seems to be that saints *persist* in faith while suffering God's absence. Mother Teresa didn't, in other words, stop believing—as that philosophy professor and I did—even though she no longer heard God's voice or sensed the divine will leading her. Instead, she redoubled her efforts on behalf of the unwanted. She continued to teach what she knew about Jesus and strove, her own darkness notwithstanding, to impart his light to the world. In view of her dogged perseverance as a believer with so little enjoyment of God's company, I was inclined to agree with Father Brian Kolodiejchuk, the priest who argued for Teresa's beatification and edited *Come Be My Light*, that, despite her frequent declarations of faithlessness, "She did have faith, a biblical faith, a blind faith, a faith that had been tried and tested in the furnace of suffering, and that traced the path to Him through darkness. Undeterred by feelings, she continued living by the faith she felt as lost."

The Catholic Church is right, I think, to interpret such perseverance in believing while suffering God's apparent absence as evidence of great faith. No longer sensing God's presence, dark night sufferers depend, as Teresa says, on "blind faith" to keep on believing. Blind faith—the very faith demanded of all of us who missed out on Jesus' first coming to our world and must wait for the second in order to see and hear and touch God—is the greatest faith there can be. Jesus himself applauds it. He tells Thomas, "Because you have seen me, you have believed; blessed are those who have not seen and yet have believed" (John 20:29).

I need to confess, here, that, until I came to read of Mother Teresa's faith struggles, I was never much impressed with her. I've always been suspicious of celebrity believers. I force myself to think well of them and smile in agreement when others go on about them, but, deep down, I just don't trust their motives. I take to heart Jesus' repeated criticisms of those who fast or pray or do their acts of charity publicly. He routinely calls them "hypocrites." My own potential hypocrisy in writing about my faith for a public audience complicates my suspicions considerably, especially because I regard my faith writings as a way of praying. In any case, Mother Teresa's sheer fame made her, for me, suspect.

I was particularly skeptical of Mother Teresa's popular reputation as perhaps the greatest twentieth-century believer. Certainly, Teresa was an impressively selfless woman, but I had my doubts about what her charitable activities had to do with her faith. It's entirely possible to be an atheist—or a Hindu or an animist or a secular humanist or a Rotarian, and maybe even a Wiccan or a Satanist— and also be what I would call a "good" person: namely, one devoted to helping, healing, loving, or protecting those less fortunate than oneself. I know many nonbelievers who do good deeds all the time and typically with more zeal than I can usually muster. Indeed, most professing atheists I have known have been "better Christians" than

I am, if being a "good Christian" amounts to devoting oneself to the less fortunate, as many appear to believe it does. To me, Mother Teresa was like any other charitable individual: a good person, doubtless, and thus to be admired. And maybe she believed in the same God I worshipped. But I wasn't convinced of her faith, or even particularly interested in it.

Having since studied what Mother Teresa wrote of her faith and faith struggles, I've also found much that disturbs me. She had such alarming—even presumptuous—spiritual plans for herself. To be Jesus' wife. To be his mother. To lessen his suffering. "To be His Victim." To "be the one" to satiate his thirst on the cross. She vowed, on pain of eternal damnation, not to refuse God anything and undertook "to smile even at Jesus and so hide if possible the pain and the darkness of my soul even from Him." She longed to "be nobody even to God" and, yet, to "love Him as He has never been loved before." She often wrote of her own suffering as pleasing or consoling to God. And, although she did write convincingly of her agony, her jottings were also vague and disturbingly melodramatic-sounding, reminiscent of the lovelorn, stream-of-depression poetry my students were always writing and wanting me to read when I taught high school English.

I don't know how to say this without sounding faithless myself, but Mother Teresa—perhaps because, as a nun, she lived a more spiritually focused life than most of us do—seemed, from my reading, *unnaturally* preoccupied with God's absence and with her resulting darkness, loneliness, and pain. Not that I think God's absence shouldn't preoccupy a person. But consider. She traveled widely and seemed to have friends everywhere. She regularly shared her most intimate thoughts with a variety of men who clearly cared deeply about her. She lived among women who all but worshipped her. Yet, these earthly relationships seem not to have assuaged her loneliness in the least.

And then there are those denials that she had any faith at all. *Could she have actually lost her faith?* I wondered as I read her confessions. *Or never had faith to begin with?* Perhaps she was simply the manipulative hypocrite that her main detractor—her atheist counterpart in fame, Christopher Hitchens—presents her as in the book-length attack on Mother Teresa he wrote during her lifetime.[3] In a review of *Come Be My Light* entitled "Teresa, Bright and Dark,"[4] Hitchens diagnosed Mother Teresa's spiritual dilemma as "the inevitable result of a dogma that asks people to believe impossible things and then makes them feel abject and guilty when their innate reason rebels." He summed up her work as "a strenuous and almost hysterical effort to drown out the awful fear of 'absence.'" He mocked even the anguish of her letters and found in her loss of a sense of God's presence gleeful support for his own view that "the absence of evidence is evidence of absence." In another review, he dismissed her as a "fraud."[5]

Mother Teresa's *own* anxiety about being a fraud gave me pause, though. In her letters, she often fretted that others must think her a hypocrite. Hypocrisy and fraud are the sort of crimes in which intentionality is crucial, it seems to me. You can't be accidentally hypocritical or a fraud by mistake. Surely, you can't genuinely lament God's absence—and, for all their melodrama, Teresa's complaints do sound genuinely wretched—and, at the same time, pretend faith in God's presence.

Or can you? Certainly, most believers probably pretend from time to time a deeper faith than they feel—at least in public. Or, I should say, certainly I have done so. I spent years as a teenager and on into my college years, while steadily losing the faith of my childhood, not only attending church but participating in worship music and fervently praying, both privately and publicly, words that meant nothing to me. I was trying to pray and worship myself back into faith, one might argue, but, in my view, I was crassly mouthing—although in secret despair—creedal mysteries of a faith I no longer felt and that I would soon no longer even claim.

Worse, having rediscovered God since that time and developed ways of noticing God's attendance in my daily life, I have periods even now when God seems gone. Sometimes long periods—weeks, months at a time—when I don't sense God there at all. The Bible stops speaking to me—or, more accurately, I lose interest in it and stop reading. My garden stops drawing me, as it usually does, into intimacy with God. My daily run—one of my richest prayer times, because I am outside and alone—becomes another chore, filling my mind with five miles of Godless chatter. Church is suddenly boring or exasperating and I quit going. Even the cheery sweetness of fellow believers irritates me. I find myself critical of all things Christian: services, sermons, goodness, easy answers to looming questions.

Usually, there's an obvious trigger for one of these periods of God's absence from my life. My longest one coincided with my worst bout of post-traumatic stress disorder, and shorter ones have occurred when I was unhappy or anxious about some life event. Sometimes, though, spiritual dryness—or distance from or blindness to God—just comes over me without a reason. It's like falling out of the consuming passion of early love and finding oneself in the monotony of married life. No, it's worse than that. It's like falling out of love entirely—which only ever happened to me in relationships I had before I met my husband Kris. I'd be going along and abruptly realize that the guy I was with was a bore or a jerk. Just like that. *What did I see in that guy in the first place?* I'd find myself wondering.

With boyfriends, my getting to that question signaled the end of our relationship, but with God it invariably sparks a return—and often a deeper relationship than I had previously enjoyed. Having believed in God as a child, returned to faith as an adult, and sought evidence of God's presence for a lifetime, I have many answers to the question, *What did I see in God in the first place?* All of the answers that I have explored in this book, in fact. My perception of God's presence may evaporate, but my ability to sense the created world does not. The same goes for the records of God's presence found in the pages of the Bible. Like Mother Teresa, I also have clear memories of God's previous presence in my life and a long register of spiritual evidence that has persuaded me of God's loving attention over the years. Intentionally revisiting these resources with the goal of rekindling my faith not only brings me back into a sense of God's presence but intensifies my trust that, come what may, God will never actually desert me.

Although my teenage faith loss lasted well into my thirties and seemed irreversible at the time, nowadays I find it as hard to imagine being permanently outside of God's presence as to imagine being parted from my husband. Kris and I have invested a good deal in our alliance thus far—not merely mutual love but the daily sacrifices and ongoing exertions involved in joining one's life to another's. We've produced children together, we share living quarters, we combine our incomes, and we have made plans about our future together. It clearly profits us both in countless ways to stay in harmony with each other—that is, each aware of, grateful for, and dedicated to preserving the other's participation in our life. Even our differences of opinion and taste and occasional fights ultimately tighten our relationship and shape our history. Similarly, while God may drift from my perception as a result of my emotional problems or spiritual shortsightedness, God and I are by now so intertwined that I know I could not extricate myself from God without dreadful effort—even fifty years' worth of dreadful effort, I suspect, although I hardly claim the faith endurance of which Mother Teresa seems to have been capable.

After I read Mother Teresa's fragmentary record of trudging faithward through such a desert of longing and spiritual penury, I felt unexpected empathy for this celebrity believer and was convinced, although the spiritual status of another cannot be definitively known, of her deep faith. Her confessions of darkness are heartrending, her embarrassment about them even more so. Having spent the better part of her life struggling to understand her plight, she had, I suspected, important wisdom to offer fellow God-seekers about the pursuit of faith in the context of God's apparent absence. Her reflections on God's presence—not only in *Come Be My Light* but in other books on spiritual topics she published during her lifetime—are her legacy to those of us who long, if less intensely, for a clearer sense of God's presence.

Come Be My Light reveals many strategies by which Mother Teresa sought to alleviate her misery and persist in faith despite overwhelming feelings of doubt and forsakenness. One key strategy was to seek the counsel and consolation of spiritual advisers. It was evidently difficult for Mother Teresa to make herself vulnerable to others; nevertheless, she exposed her secret suffering to her advisers' scrutiny with astonishing candor. They encouraged her in faith; prayed for her; interposed their own love and attention as substitutes for God's; and offered her various helpful explanations for her predicament, such as the reminder of Jesus' own cry of forsakenness from the cross and the suggestion that she might be vicariously experiencing Jesus' presence by sharing his agony. Teresa's advisers also helped her appreciate as evidence of God's presence the considerable signs of God's favor and attention in her life, such as her mission's success and her saintly reputation throughout the world. Most importantly, perhaps, her advisers simply listened to her. Instead of making accusations or attempting to explain her darkness away, they helped her endure it.

Not all of us would be as fortunate as Teresa was in finding non-judgmental advisers determined to encourage us above all else. Still, much solace—and perhaps the special comfort of discovering that one is not alone in longing for a sense of God's presence—might be gained in risking embarrassment and seeking the counsel of the spiritually knowledgeable during periods of God's perceived absence.

Another method by which Teresa sought to endure her darkness was to record her struggles in written form. In her letters, she frequently mentions her inability to pray and even to speak at all, but she seems to have had no difficulty recording her feelings during those years. She wrote hastily and frankly, wasting little worry on how her words might be understood—or misunderstood—by others and even less on the form her writings took. She capitalized and punctuated according to her own whims. One senses, in reading her dashed fragments of thought, a crushing sort of relief, a sighing, as though she were telling her advisers—and God and herself—"There. Now I've said it. Now perhaps this wretchedness will leave me." My experience as a writing teacher has shown me that writing has this effect on many. For this reason, psychologists often give their patients writing assignments. Writing can be a release, almost an exorcism, freeing the writer from impediments to growth and healing.

Writing also focuses the writer's attention on important concerns or aspects of a problem of which the writer may not have been aware. Reading back through my first forays into creative writing, for example, I find that most of my stories had to do with finding and losing faith, although I didn't know that I was concerned with anything to do with God at the time. What I did know was that writing sustained me and gave substance to my longings. Later, when I came to believe in God again, writing was also where I took my questions and doubts. Thus, writing served as the road for my faith journey, both in the darkness of unbelief and in the light of hope, and the resulting records of that journey reveal God's presence along the way. I'm guessing the same may have been true for Mother Teresa. Having recorded the longing and darkness and pain she suffered in God's absence alongside her dogged conviction that God nevertheless not only existed but loved her, Teresa created an all too convincing testimony, not unlike those of the biblical psalmists, of what it is like to be separated from God, as, in some sense, we all are in this life.

In fact, Mother Teresa's fragmentary letters sound very much like the Psalms, which often begin with complaints of distress and anguished pleas for God's presence and then end with affirmations of faith. Reading Teresa's writings resolved, for me, what had previously seemed an almost schizophrenic-sounding incongruity in the Psalms. *How could the psalmists complain bitterly that God was not present, not listening, and then, in the next sentence, claim confidence that God was taking care of them?* I always wondered. Somehow, Mother Teresa's lamenting—even protesting—God's absence bridged for me the dark hole between despair and faith.

Mother Teresa's insights into how she managed to survive as a believer while suffering God's apparent absence evolved, during her years of spiritual dearth, from desperate soul-barings into cheery directives she repeatedly offered others and eventually into a sophisticated philosophy of God's presence and a believer's perception of it. "Nothing can make us holy," she writes, "except the presence of God . . . . And for me, the presence of God lies in fidelity to the little things."[6] She recommends that we "not waste our time in looking for extraordinary experiences" but, rather, "Always be faithful in little things, for in them our strength lies."[7] In other words, one's spiritual strength lies not in extraordinary experiences of God's presence—such as Jesus' speaking directly to Teresa and asking her to come be his light—but in the little, day-to-day activities of faith.

These "little things" might loom large to us, especially in light of Teresa's enormous charitable exertions. In her Nobel Peace Prize acceptance speech,[8] though, she put what she meant in perspective. "When I pick up a person from the street, hungry," she said, "I give him a plate of rice, a piece of bread, I have satisfied. I have removed that hunger." Offering food to the starving was, for her, a little thing. In the wealthy West, though, she pointed out, hunger is not for food but for company and love—for the sheer presence of others in the lives of the unwanted. She recounted visiting an affluent nursing home "where they had all these old parents of sons and daughters who had just put them in an institution and forgotten" them. Every eye was on the door. The little thing called for, she suggested, was the simple presence of those sons and daughters.

Similarly, she spoke of "young boys and girls given into drugs" because, in their homes, there was "no one in the family to receive them." She challenged her listeners to "find the poor"—that is, Jesus himself—in their own lives simply by being there. She described her mission work as keeping company with Jesus himself: "For we are touching the Body of Christ twenty-four hours. We have twenty-four hours in this presence, and so you and I." Enjoying God's presence, in short, means being present oneself—to one another and thereby to God.

She also lamented to her Nobel audience that, "if we all look into our own homes, how difficult we find it sometimes to smile at each other." To Teresa, smiling was another "little thing" essential to evoking God's presence: "Holy souls sometimes undergo great inward trial, and they know darkness. But if we want others to become aware of the presence of Jesus, we must be the first ones convinced of it."[9] In her private writings, she vowed repeatedly to smile, despite her suffering. Her primary strategy for being Jesus' light to the unwanted was to search them out in their dark holes and just smile at them. When called upon to mediate interpersonal conflicts—which, as Mother Superior to a burgeoning community of sisters, she frequently was—she typically recommended simply smiling. Will yourself to emanate joy, she seemed to be saying, and perhaps you will experience joy yourself—and with it the confidence of God's company. "Joy is a sign of union with God—of God's presence," she summarized in *The Joy in Loving: A Guide to Daily Living*.[10]

Teresa projected the joy she was determined to express into a future existence in which God would no longer be invisible, inaudible, intangible. She described eternal life as "where our soul goes to God, to be in the presence of God, to see God, to speak to God,"[11] but in this life, she preached,[13] we must remind ourselves that, without God's presence, we ourselves would not even exist: "'In him we live and move and have our being' (Acts 17:28 NAB). It is He who gives life to all, who gives power and being to all that exists. But for His sustaining presence, all things would cease to be and fall back into nothingness." God's presence is thus bound up in our own existence. Teresa characterized this human-divine interconnectedness in language reminiscent of a fetus gestating in its mother's uterus: "Consider that you are in God, surrounded and encompassed by God, swimming in God."

Indeed, God's imperceptibility might be read, she seemed to be reasoning, as a simple problem of point of view. If one is *in* God, one's perception of God's presence is shaped by that interiority. The fetus's perception of the presence of the mother is limited to sensory experiences other than seeing, hearing, touching, smelling, or tasting—at least as far as we understand the five senses with which we perceive presence *after* we are born. The fetus perceives enclosure and safety, perhaps. The euphoria of being contained in something more powerful and in charge.

I'm not sure whether memory really extends as far backward as the womb or if my toddling daughters were just especially good at imagining what the interior of a uterus might have been like, but, when each girl started talking, she told me that her experience inside of me had been of warm, wet, happy darkness. Mother Teresa's description of being "in God, surrounded and encompassed by God, swimming in God" evokes a similar experience of God's presence.

God is also within the believer—which, as I said earlier, makes it somewhat difficult for the believer to sense God's presence, since the concept of "presence" in general is the perception of that which one is not. In another twisting of point of view, Mother Teresa argued that, while God may be invisible to *us*, that does not mean *we* are invisible to *God*. She prayed,

> O God, we firmly believe that we are in your most
> holy presence,
> we believe that you see us.
> —and that at this moment you behold even the
> inmost recesses of our hearts.
> Penetrated with this your divine presence, we adore
> you.[13]

God's presence, here, manifests itself in the reality that God sees us, even sees inside of us, and thus penetrates our very consciousness.

Teresa's greatest feat in tackling her darkness was to rethink the aching absence of God as something positive. She willed herself to see her own sense of forsakenness as an intimate experience of God's love. "I accept whatever He gives and I give whatever He takes," she wrote again and again, suggesting that the loss of God's presence amounts to divine intervention. She had not *lost* her sense of God's presence; God had *taken* it. Thus, the very absence of God was proof of God's interactive presence.

It's a mystery to me how Mother Teresa maintained such confidence while suffering from the conviction that God had abandoned and did not want her, but I have decided to think of her the way I think of all believers: as a work in progress. Certainly, Teresa had much spiritual wisdom to offer us as a result of her extraordinary life of charity. Nevertheless, saint or not, she was, like all of us, messed up in many ways. In my mind, I play at diagnosing her problems, spiritual and emotional. She surely worked too hard. She was too used up to have any room left for God's presence. She was hamstrung by the crazy vows she was perpetually making. Perhaps, as some have suggested, Mother Teresa suffered from depression. Or perhaps, after receiving Jesus' personal call to come be his light, she experienced something like the aftermath of the "camp high" much discussed at the Christian summer camp my daughters used to attend. As soon as campers reentered the humdrum and conflicts of daily life, their hyperconsciousness of God in their lives waned.

As arrogant as it sounds, I like to fantasize about what *I* would have advised Mother Teresa to do or think about her situation had *I* been one of her spiritual advisers. A biblical studies professor at my university once commanded a student who couldn't pray to just stop trying. He gave the student a time frame—months, I think it was—and, for that long, he forbade her to pray. Cured her in a heartbeat. I might have given Mother Teresa a similar directive: "I forbid you to even think about God's presence for the next five years. If the desire for God's company comes into your mind, go have coffee with a friend. Or read a novel. Or take a walk."

Or I'd have reminded her of Jesus' promise: "Ask and it will be given to you; seek and you will find; knock and the door will be opened to you. For everyone who asks receives; those who seek find; and to those who knock, the door will be opened" (Matthew 7:7–8).

"If God's not there," I might have told her, "then perhaps you aren't really seeking, knocking, asking." We could have talked about that possibility. Or devoted a decade of correspondence to sorting it out.

Come Be My Light includes, as an appendix, a spiritual self-examination worksheet that Teresa responded to during a two-week retreat ten years into her ministry. In one response, she identified her "dangerous occasions of mortal sin" as, simply, *"my eyes."* She described herself in the next question as *"harsh and quick. Inclined to look,"* so, by considering her eyes sources of sin, she may have been referring to a tendency to be overcritical of others. Still, I wondered after reading her self-appraisal if she might not have been referencing Jesus' cryptic words about darkness within: "The eye is the lamp of the body. If your eyes are healthy, your whole body will be full of light. But if your eyes are unhealthy, your whole body will be full of darkness. If then the light within you is darkness, how great is that darkness!" (Matthew 6:22–23). I'd like to have discussed that passage with Mother Teresa. Maybe, together, we could have gotten to the bottom of what in the world it might mean—for her, for me, for us all.

Perhaps I'd have reminded Mother Teresa of how she herself once described the pursuit of God's presence as being "constantly available to Him, loving Him with our whole heart, whole mind, whole soul, and whole strength, no matter in what form He may come to us."[14]

Maybe God was coming to her in a form she didn't recognize. Or one she couldn't allow.

"Maybe God comes to you in the little things you get back," I would have suggested, "not just the ones you give. Not just the smile you give, but the one you get. Not the body of Christ you touch, but the hand that touches *you*."

I'd like to have touched her. Smiled at her. Gotten to know her. I'd like to have cooked a really good meal for her. Charlotte's favorite, chicken pot pie. The honey-glazed carrots speckled with chives that Lulu loves. Or a sweet-sour salad of cucumbers, onions, tomatoes, and feta cheese.

I am positive Mother Teresa's problem was solvable.

———————

1 ✤ Approach someone to be your spiritual adviser. Select someone whose religious views you share and who is more experienced than you are as a believer. Reassure the person that you won't be hurt or offended if he or she declines, and *don't* be hurt or offended. If the person agrees, establish a regular time to meet and maybe a schedule of events that you can imagine happening: praying together, discussing an agreed upon passage of scripture, researching a particular spiritual issue or question. Don't regard the person as your therapist or monopolize your time together talking about your personal problems, although these will surely come up. Instead, focus specifically on your spiritual life and growth.

2 ✤ Record your feelings about God's apparent absence as bluntly as you can. Allow yourself to be as angry or hurt or

confused or slighted as you actually feel. If your feelings toward God—or your loss of a sense of God's presence—is related to an incident of loss or sorrow, tell that story and hold God accountable for it.

3 ❧ Read through what you wrote in the last exercise as well as your spiritual journal and any of the other exercises that you have completed in this book. Look for repeated themes and words or expressions. These clues about your inner life—which you may not have been aware of—can be a significant help to you in solving the problem of God's absence. Use what you discover as a point of focus in attempting to enter God's presence. It may be that forgiveness is in order. Or that a problem parent or a church experience has perverted your view of God, thus preventing you from truly desiring God's presence. Meditate on what you find and pray for deliverance from your own preoccupations so that you can allow yourself to enjoy God's company.

4 ❧ Compose a list of "little things" you might do that might help you experience your faith more intimately. Resolve to smile at some unlovable person in your acquaintance. Make a special effort to be present in the life of someone you know who feels unwanted. Establish a tradition or habit of granting your full presence to those who long for it—your children, your spouse, your ailing mother-in-law. Schedule time with the person and plan an activity—such as playing a game or preparing an after-school snack—that specifically shows that you love the person.

5 ❧ In Genesis 32, Jacob wrestles with God—referred to as a man in parts of the narrative—a whole night long and, even

though his thigh is injured during the fight, Jacob refuses to let go until God blesses him. Afterward, he receives a new name, Israel (which means, He Struggles with God), because, as the man says, "you have struggled with God and with human beings and have overcome" (Genesis 32:28). Activate faith in your search for God's presence by rethinking your sense of God's absence as something positive, if painful, and divinely orchestrated for your benefit. How might your struggles as a believer actually be moving you closer to God?

CHAPTER FIFTEEN

Could God Actually Be Absent?

ONE SUNDAY, in the fellowship gathering following the service at a church I attended early on as an adult believer, an elder stridently objected to one of the praise songs we had sung that morning as "theologically incorrect." His complaint perplexed me. The song was Keith Green's "Create in Me a Clean Heart,"[1] which I had become acquainted with only a few months earlier at a women's retreat that had used the song as its theme. So, although I was as yet scripturally illiterate in those early days of my faith, as chance would have it I knew that Green's lyrics were taken almost verbatim from the King James Version of one of the Psalms, where, having committing adultery with Bathsheba, David begs,

> Create in me a clean heart, O God; and renew a right
> spirit within me.
> Cast me not away from thy presence; and take not
> thy holy spirit from me.
> Restore unto me the joy of thy salvation; and uphold
> me with thy free spirit. (51: 10–12)

At the retreat, I had loved the plaintive song and months later was still singing David's prayer as if it were my own. Indeed, it was my own. Only a year or two after my return to faith, my initial excitement about God—that is, the joy of God's salvation, as I understood David's words to mean—had already begun to dissolve into a sort of spiritual oblivion. Somehow, unintentionally, I lost track of God from one Sunday to the next and found myself devising strategies—such as that retreat—for regaining my original enthusiasm about my newfound faith.

David's prayer also gave words to a fear I'd had ever since becoming a believer as an adult: that God might go missing *again*, as in my teenage years, and leave me once again bereft and empty. *Cast me not away from thy presence, O God*, I had pleaded along with David throughout the retreat and then again, with the special fervor that always accompanies meaningful songs that reemerge from my past, on that Sunday morning in church. *Take not thy Holy Spirit from me!*

The objectionable song and I had a history, in other words, so I wasn't just being smug or contradictory—although I'm given to both failings—when I countered the elder's pronouncement with the demand to know how the song could be theologically incorrect when it was taken directly from the Bible.

The elder explained that David's plea that God not take the Holy Spirit away from him was no longer relevant for New Testament believers, since Jesus had promised that, after he returned to heaven, God would send the Holy Spirit to be with us always.

The elder's explanation should have satisfied me, especially after I made him show me where exactly, in scripture, Jesus made this promise. But, even after reading Jesus' red-lettered words to his disciples from the much annotated page of the man's Bible—"And I will pray the Father, and he shall give you another Comforter, that he may abide with you for ever" (John 14:16 KJV)—and after verifying that Jesus had said the same thing in my own Bible, I still wasn't convinced.

After all, I reasoned, I'd been a New Testament believer myself as a child, before I ever lost my faith. I had trusted, in the unquestioning way of children that Jesus so often applauded, that the scriptural stories I'd learned in my Catholic youth were the truth. I had sincerely believed God's son had become a human being and died for my sins and risen alive and that, as a result, I would someday go to heaven. I had directed my juvenile prayers to God the Father, the Son, and the Holy Spirit, according not only to Catholic tradition but my own utter acceptance of a God made manifest in all three persons of the Trinity.

Even as I passed from the faith of my childhood into the unbelief of my later years, it never seemed to me that I'd had any hand in God's ensuing absence from my life. I never willfully left God's presence, as I soon left the presence of my earthly parents and siblings and compatriots to live abroad. Many years after my faith had left me entirely—indeed, throughout the entire twenty years of my atheism—I still longed for God. I yearned to hear God's voice, to sense God listening to my prayers and inhabiting the odd church I happened into, and to trust—oh, to be able to trust!—that the God of all creation not only existed but cared about me in particular and even then, though imperceptibly, was accompanying me on my journey through life. For what seemed, in retrospect, like eternity itself, I had strained to believe. But God was gone. That much I knew. And, for years after my faith returned to me, I still struggled to reassure myself—or to let my husband or others who seemed theologically knowledgeable or, best of all, Jesus himself reassure me—that this disaster would never happen again.

"Once saved, always saved," many fellow Christians told me. I was reading the Bible regularly by then, though, and, while I did find some support there for my friends' confidence that believers could not lose their salvation, I also found many biblical episodes—from the moment Adam and Eve were cast from the Garden of Eden to the Flood right up to the final condemnation of a great many to an eternity outside of God's presence—that seemed to challenge that guarantee. *Were there no one-time believers among them?* I marveled. I read with particular uneasiness the stories of Aaron's priestly sons and the ill-fated Ark-carrier Uzzah, Old Testament believers who'd suffered instantaneous death for what seemed to me to be mere breaches of protocol.

"That was under the Law," my Christian friends tried to reassure me. "In the New Testament, things are different."

But the account of Ananias and Sapphira, New Testament believers similarly dealt with for lying about their resources while donating money to the apostles, filled me with dread. What if *I* were summarily banished from God's presence for some misstep, as Ananias and Sapphira appear to have been?

Anticipating this possibility, I complained, along with my banished ancestor Cain, in a heartfelt prayer of preemption. "My punishment is more than I can bear," I told God, as though the imagined expulsion had already occurred. "Today you are driving me from the land, and I will be hidden from your presence; I will be a restless wanderer on the earth, and whoever finds me will kill me" (Genesis 4:13–14). God's response to Cain—a mark of protection against any would-be killers—offered meager comfort. In the end, we're told, "Cain went out from the LORD's presence and lived in the land of Nod, east of Eden" (Genesis 4:16)—a place apparently inhabited by people for whom God was perpetually absent.

And God, if the truth be told, is frequently absent in scripture. Or so it seems. The psalmists are always complaining about it. I Samuel 3 opens with the comment that "In those days the word of the LORD was rare; there were not many visions." There's a gaping silence of four hundred years between the Testaments, and, although Luke reassures us in Acts that God "is not far from any one of us" (17:27), in the same breath he describes all of human history as a desperate groping after God, reminiscent of the one Amos describes:

> "The days are coming," declares the Sovereign LORD,
> "when I will send a famine through the land—
> not a famine of food or a thirst for water,
> but a famine of hearing the words of the LORD.
>
> "People will stagger from sea to sea
> and wander from north to east,
> searching for the word of the LORD,
> but they will not find it.
>
> "In that day
> the lovely young women and strong young men
> will faint because of thirst." (Amos 8:11–13)

I was like the young women Amos mentions—not lovely, perhaps, but thirsty for God's voice. As Amos prophesied, I'd staggered from sea to sea and wandered the world, hungry for God.

And even after I rediscovered God, I yet hungered and thirsted on occasion. On frequent occasion. Despite the fervor of my renewed faith, despite my fresh confidence that God not only existed but loved me and interacted with me on a regular basis, I nevertheless worried that I might be among those who, at the end of time, will cry, "Lord, Lord, did we not prophesy in your name and in your name drive out demons and in your name perform many miracles?"—those to whom Jesus will say, "'I never knew you. Away from me, you evildoers!" (Matthew 7:22–23).

Unknown to God. Cast away. Spirit-less. Alone in an infinity of woe.

Contemplating these eventualities, I've devoted much spiritual research since those days to convincing myself that the God I loved in childhood and lost in my teens and found again as an adult really would stay with me this time, for *all* time, just as Jesus promises.

Go with me, for a moment, to one of those years of God's absence from my life. I was living at the time in West Berlin, one of a series of cities to which I fled in the aftermath of the central catastrophes of my youth: my mother's struggle with cancer, my family's ensuing wreckage, and a sexual assault when I was in graduate school. I'd spent a year in Berlin previously, studying at the university there and pursuing a relationship with a German boyfriend. We'd shared an apartment with a childhood friend of his and spent our evenings in the company of other hometown friends of theirs who were studying in Berlin to avoid military duty, from which West Berliners were exempt. With these fellow outsiders, I'd spent an entertaining year sharing meals, discussing German politics, listening to jazz, playing cards, and drinking beer and shooting pool in our neighborhood pub. After that year, I remembered Berlin as a place where I'd been surrounded by friends and was always doing something exciting. So, it made sense, when the world in which I found myself became intolerable, to go back there.

This time, though, I was all by myself. I got jobs teaching English and rented an apartment far from my old circle of friends in an outlying district of Berlin populated by workers and fellow foreigners. That year was the loneliest year of my life. Except for my students and the strangers who sold me bread and cheese and vegetables, I spoke to no one. My Berlin friends, older now and settled into jobs, were rarely available, and the time we did spend together was complicated by a marked lack of spontaneity due to the long subway rides I had to take to get to their part of town. Or so I told myself. It took some time for me to realize that my old friends simply didn't like being with me anymore.

"You're not fun, like you used to be," one of them told me.

"You're angry all the time," another said.

Indeed, I made an enemy of yet another friend—a man who, by chance, lived in my new neighborhood—because I had decided, in a fit of wrath about some ill-worded comment, that he was a misogynist.

I was going through a period then when I was prone to outbursts at the least provocation. I blew up at salespeople and anyone who crossed me. I despised police officers and others in minor positions of authority. The few fellow Americans I encountered enraged me. I stomped the streets of Berlin brooding with anger—at drunks asleep on subway benches, at revelers marching the streets after soccer games, at people who didn't walk fast enough to suit me. I hated men. Most of all, I hated men who hated women—just as (I see this now, but didn't then) the men who had held me up and sexually assaulted me hated women.

I was, in short, depressed: steeped in rage and, beneath the rage, in a misery of forsakenness. Everyone had deserted me, it seemed. I felt abandoned and unloved. As a result, I really *was* no fun to be with, and my friends were wise to avoid me. But the problem was not that anyone had left *me*. Rather, I had left *them*. And I didn't love them. I was too caught up in my own rage and hurt to love anyone.

This paradox—of being unlovable and thus feeling unloved, of forsaking and thus feeling forsaken—is, I think, what losing track of God comes down to. David attributed his own fear of abandonment, evident in his plea that God not cast him out or take away the Holy Spirit, to his own sin of adultery.

"Create in me a clean heart," he pleaded, probably reasoning—if he was like me—that, if he were clean-hearted, then he would be love-worthy, and if he were love-worthy, God would never leave him. But the reality is that no one is wholly love-worthy. And, if we make ourselves unlovable—through hate or anger or selfishness or greed—then *we* are the ones who do the leaving. Not God. God marks believers with a protective sign, and the Holy Spirit dogs our heels, nudging us back into step with the Father, reminding us of the Son's advice, choreographing the minutiae of our lives into a spiritual dance that demands nothing more complicated from us than the desire to live and move and have our being in its rhythm. That's the sort of perpetual attendance that Jesus is talking about when he promises us a comforter—or a counselor or an advocate, as other versions of the Bible translate the word. Or, as the passage goes on to say, the "Spirit of truth" that lives with us and in us (John 14:17).

That elder at my old church would simplify my words here to say that God does not leave us, but, rather, we leave God through sin. To sin is to leave God's presence, he would say, and to enjoy God's presence is to quit sinning. And the elder would no doubt be right. But this explanation argues that we can control God's presence. It also conjures a God whose only remedies for our unacceptable behavior are to leave or go silent in disapproval. Absenting oneself and using silence to express displeasure are, to my mind, dysfunctional solutions, as when a teenager slams the bedroom door or when a husband responds to his wife's accusations with implacable silence. Silence and absence are bids for power when one feels powerless. In healthy relationships, people don't just disappear or go silent in disapproval when there's a problem. And if there were ever someone who operates in the realm of health, I'm guessing it's the one who created life and health in the first place.

More important, though, if we argue that not sensing God's presence simply means we're sinning, then we are ignoring a perceptual dilemma of those suffering God's absence. When a person longs, in vain, for God's presence, it simply doesn't *feel* like sin—that is, one doesn't feel as though one has committed a crime.

Perhaps the problem is that we tend to think about sin as a specific action. To sin, we often think, is to intentionally disobey some specific rule. Thou shalt not murder. Thou shalt not covet. Thou shalt not hate God. The sins I have committed in my past, it seems to me, are much subtler than that—and thus more insidious.

Sin is described throughout the Bible in terms of the verb *turn*. Sinners *turn* away from God. Others *turn* them from God's way. They *turn* to idolatry. Biblical writers also use the verb *turn* to prescribe the sinner's recourse when God seems gone: Simply *turn* away from sin and *turn* back to God. The verb *turn*, among its many definitions—my dictionary lists thirty-one—means to focus on or train one's attention or interest onto something. To pay attention to something new. To notice. Sin, it seems to me, amounts to an error of notice. Being out of God's presence is not punishment for sin. Rather, it is the natural result of turning away from God and redirecting one's notice elsewhere.

I have come to trust in the believer's "eternal security," as I learned to call the notion of once saved, always saved. Jesus asserts that "whoever comes to me I will never drive away.... For my Father's will is that everyone who looks to the Son and believes in him shall have eternal life, and I will raise them up at the last day" (John 6:37, 40). Jesus also reassures the crowds, repeating himself for emphasis, that those who believe "shall never perish; no one will snatch them out of my hand. My Father, who has given them to me, is greater than all; no one can snatch them out of my Father's hand"

(John 10:28–29). Reading these words now, I am confident that, had I died an unbeliever at twenty, I would now be in heaven, because in my childhood I had believed in the one God had sent.

But having eternal life after my earthly death and enjoying a consciousness of God's company in the meantime are not, to my mind, the same thing. Protected though believers are against eternal misery, they may nevertheless turn away in despair and wander out of God's presence during their lives on earth. They may, as Mother Teresa apparently did, suffer a sense of God's absence for many years. They may feel abandoned or cast out of God's presence. God may seem to disappear from their lives, as happened once to me.

Here is a comfort for those who suffer—as I did and, on occasion, still do—from the notion that God has left them. As the Israelites neared the Promised Land, God gave Aaron and his sons formal instruction on how to bless the people: "Say to them,

> 'The LORD bless you
> and keep you;
>
> 'the LORD make his face shine on you
> and be gracious to you;
>
> 'the LORD turn his face toward you
> and give you peace.'
> (Numbers 6:23–26)

Through the death of God's Son, we merit this blessing always: The Lord keeps us, shines all around us, inclines an ear in our direction, and turns toward us, no matter what we do. We simply need to have faith in God's ongoing presence—discerned through the efforts of the ever-present Holy Spirit—and learn how to pay attention.

But it will never be easy. Even Moses—who witnessed many

miraculous signs of God's presence, conversed with God as with a fellow human, and alone in the Old Testament was granted the opportunity to see God directly—struggled to trust that God would not abandon him. When God promised him, "My Presence will go with you, and I will give you rest," Moses responded, "If your Presence does not go with us, do not send us up from here. How will anyone know that you are pleased with me and with your people unless you go with us?" (Exodus 33:14–16). No matter how hard God tried to convince Moses, promising him, "I will do the very thing you have asked . . . I am pleased with you . . . I know you by name" (Exodus 33:17), Moses still felt alone. And no matter how much sensory evidence Moses witnessed—the burning bush, the pillars of cloud and fire, God's thirst-quenching voice, and miracles wrought through Moses' own body—he still struggled to believe that God was really *with* him.

Having believed as an adult for over a decade now, I still pray with David, "Cast me not away from thy presence, O God; and take not thy holy spirit from me." My voice still thickens with emotion whenever, in a church service or on the radio, I sing along with that old song by Keith Green. I still long for God. Often. I still find myself feeling alone sometimes. Bit by bit, though, I have learned to check my sense of abandonment and turn my attention Godward. And each time I do, I am rewarded with a glimpse, or a murmur, or a fleeting consciousness of that invisible arm resting on my shoulder.

———————

I ❧ In a radio interview with widows I once listened to, the widows reported feeling as though they lost not only a spouse but other important relationships as well. Friends and church members and even their own children expected them to get over the loss sooner than they did and gradually stopped calling or inquiring after them. Others' responses to their grief enraged them. To a woman, they reported feeling lonely and abandoned. In the view of the people around them, by contrast, it was the widows who had quit the scene.

Consider the difficult moments of your life: when a beloved one died or some other disaster occurred, when you were depressed, when you lapsed into some behavior you knew wasn't good for you as a way of dealing with or avoiding a problem. Try to remember—or, better yet, get others who were around during your difficulty to tell you themselves—how the difficulty affected your relations with others. Did you withdraw, talk less or avoid difficult subjects, avoid or resist physical contact? Did you become angry, cold, or distant? Did you reject others' offers of help or comfort? Consider, too, others' responses to your pain. Did they withdraw from you in hurt or disapproval or anger of their own. Did they, over time, seem to abandon you to your misery? What might you have done—or, what did you do—to remedy the problem? Did you rebuild the relationship in some way? Did time alone alleviate your difficulty and allow you to let others back into your life? Reflect upon the implications of these experiences in the context of your relationship with God. Might God's absence be a manifestation of your own emotional absence? If so, what steps might you take to restore your relationship with God to the level of intimacy you once enjoyed?

2 ❧ Psychologist John Gottman studied thousands of married couples and discovered patterns in how partners relate to each other that predicted—with 94 percent accuracy—which

marriages would succeed and which fail. In *Why Marriages Succeed or Fail: And How You Can Make Yours Last*, Gottman identifies one destructive pattern as "stonewalling," observable in his subjects' silence, muttering, changing the subject, or leaving in a conflict.[2]

Examine your own marriage and other ongoing relationships for evidence of such stonewalling. If you use any of these behaviors with those you care about, you may be using them with God too. Devise strategies—practice them in your relationships with others as well as with God—for changing whichever ones you use into more healthy expressions of dissatisfaction. If you go silent, force yourself to speak. If you mutter, allow yourself—as the prophets sometimes did—to get good and angry and express your anger directly. Create opportunities for talking about difficult topics with those concerned; plan and schedule such conversations. Commit yourself to staying in relationship—and undertake healthy activities that allow you to do so—with important others and with God.

3 ⚘ Take another lesson from the psalmists: Write out prayers of misery and complaint in which you describe your pain and loss. Remember, the experience of loss is an affirmation of the worth of the lost thing. Describe your loss so completely and specifically that it honors the having. Similarly, describe your pain so completely that your imagined reader must acknowledge the great gifts of health and joy. Be honest and thorough. Do not exaggerate—as, for example, Esau exaggerates in describing his hunger to Jacob on the occasion when he sells his inheritance for a bowl of lentil soup (Genesis 25:29–34).

Finally, *whether you feel you believe what I'm asking you to write next or not*, tack onto the end of your description of loss and/or pain a declaration of faith in a God who addresses the specific pain and/or restores the particular loss that you are struggling with. Address God directly and be as specific and imaginative as you can with respect to your current pains and losses. Use a form of the verb that presents the action you speak of as already completed, even though it is not—as in, "You *brought* my father back to life" or "Your touch *has restored* feeling to my hand." You may feel as though you are lying. In fact, you will be lying, as far as your awareness of reality is concerned. Call it fiction, if lying really bothers you, but give words to your wildest hopes of repair to your pain and loss and—this is important—do so in a way that claims faith in a God who, like an ideal parent, listens to and cares for you and wants to respond favorably.

4 ❧ In the prologue to this book, I talked about my mother-in-law's notion that God leaves her when she hasn't been paying enough attention. For her, paying attention involves reading scripture, noticing the blessings she enjoys, and thanking God in prayer. She remedies God's absence by devoting more time to these activities and by simply, as she says, "telling God I need him." Sometimes, when we look for solutions to a problem, we fail to see the simplest and most obvious one. Develop the habit of praying for God to be present to you. Even if God doesn't immediately show up in response to your prayer—as my mother-in-law reports God does for her—you will have at least turned your face in God's direction.

CHAPTER SIXTEEN

Embracing Hope

HE OTHER DAY IN CHURCH, I heard again the amusing story of Jacob, that self-serving finagler most Bible readers have to struggle to like, waking up in the desert from a dream about angels on a stairway to heaven and saying to himself, "Surely the LORD is in this place, and I was not aware of it" (Genesis 28:16). As always when I unexpectedly encounter a favorite or especially relevant passage of scripture, I noticed different details than I ever had before and also felt as though God had spoken the words personally to me. This time I was struck by the promise God made to Jacob in his dream: "I am with you and will watch over you wherever you go, and I will bring you back to this land. I will not leave you until I have done what I have promised you" (28:15).

Echoing behind God's pledge of presence I heard the similar reassurances of God's son, heralded as God With Us, the physical embodiment of God's promise. "I will not leave you as orphans," Jesus assured his disciples (John 14:18), even as he discussed his imminent death. He told them that, after he returned to his father, he would send another comforter and advocate, the Holy Spirit, who would be with them—and, by extension, with us—forever. He was then executed and buried, only to emerge live from his tomb and walk again among his disciples for a while. And, not long before "he was taken up before their very eyes, and a cloud hid him from their sight" (Acts 1:9), he reassured them yet again: "And surely I am with you always, to the very end of the age" (Matthew 28:20).

Such soothing promises for the spiritually famished. God's perpetual, albeit invisible, presence. The continuing comfort, guidance, and advocacy of the Holy Spirit. The enduring attendance of God With Us, even after he has quit this world and returned to heaven. These assurances of divine company and attendance, I realized as I listened to God's promise to stay with Jacob, encapsulate all of scripture for those of us who seek God.

Consider. God walked with Adam and Eve in the Garden and interacted with many of their descendents even after they sinned and sought to hide themselves. To Moses, God promised, "My presence will go with you" (Exodus 33:14), and to Joshua, "As I was with Moses, so I will be with you; I will never leave you nor forsake you" (Joshua 1:5). God told Solomon, at the consecration of the temple in Jerusalem, "My eyes and my heart will always be there" (I Kings 9:3). The psalmists portray God as a shield, a refuge for the oppressed, a watchful shepherd who not only looks after the sheep but dwells among them. In Jesus' stories, we see God as the host of a great banquet who invites strangers off the streets when the invited guests are too busy to attend. God is also the owner of a hundred sheep who goes after the one that wanders away from the flock and a doting father who searches the horizon in hope that his absent son will return. The "poor and needy"—those who, as Mother Teresa pointed out, are routinely forgotten and abandoned by the world—are specifically included in God's assurances: "I, the God of Israel, will not forsake them," God tells Isaiah (Isaiah 41:17).

Sometimes, especially in the Old Testament, the promise of God's presence seems contingent upon righteous behavior. The writer of 2 Chronicles warns, "If you seek him, he will be found by you, but if you forsake him, he will forsake you" (15:2). But even that grim prophecy holds a promise to every seeker: God longs to be found by us. "You will seek me and find me when you seek me with all your heart. I will be found by you," God told the exiled Israelites (Jeremiah 29:13–14), and Jesus reiterated this promise to his disciples and to the crowds of people he attracted wherever he went: "Ask and it will be given to you; seek and you will find; knock and the door will be opened to you. For everyone who asks receives; those who seek find; and to those who knock, the door will be opened" (Luke 11:9–10 and Matthew 7:7–8). In Revelation, John gives us a preview of that moment of discovery, when the "ruler of God's creation" will cry, "Here I am! I stand at the door and knock. If anyone hears my voice and opens the door, I will come in and eat with them, and they with me" (3:14, 20).

In fact, the entire human story, from creation to the end of time, can be understood as the playing out of God's desire to be found, as Paul argues in his famous speech to the people of Athens assembled at Mars Hill to hear the latest ideas. "From one man he made all the nations," Paul explained, "that they should inhabit the whole earth; and he marked out their appointed times in history and the boundaries of their lands. God did this so that they would seek him and perhaps reach out for him and find him, though he is not far from any one of us" (Acts 17:26–27). Interestingly, in this synopsis of God's plan for humankind, seeking God and *reaching out for* God—or, as other translations phrase it, *feeling after* or *groping for* God—are *not* synonymous enterprises. One might long for and even aimlessly seek but perhaps *not* actually reach out for and thus find God—who, ironically, hovers near each one of us. Taking the step from passive longing into more proactive and effectual *groping* for God is the essence of faith. As long as we do the "work of God"—that is, as Jesus defines it, "to believe in the one he has sent" (John 6:26)—then we may be confident of God's company *after* we die. In the meantime, though, unless we continue to grope and feel after and reach out for God, we risk denying ourselves all sense of the abiding presence God promises.

I remember my adult reentry into faith as a stepping forth, from decades of an almost unconscious seeking, into a more determined and hopeful and sometimes scary pursuit of God. It was a process of revelation not unlike my learning how to snorkel. Without thinking much about what I wanted to be able to see underwater in the first place, I initially spent my time in the water practicing breathing through the mouthpiece and experimenting with how much weight I needed to wear on my belt to get below the surface. Soon, I was paddling around in the shallows peering through my mask at the tide pool creatures scuttling around my feet.

Then one day I took a real diving trip out to Catalina Island on a friend's boat. Somewhere between the invisible coastline we had left behind us and the unseen island before us, we dropped into the ocean, and, before I knew what was happening, my friend disappeared and I found myself alone in a murky forest of giant kelp wavering up from the darkness below. It took everything in me to make myself enter that blackness, kicking myself forward and parting the kelp with my hands, and I worried the whole time. *What if I'm lost? What if I can't find my way back to the boat? What if I suddenly forget how to breathe through this awkward tube and start to drown? Why did I ever want to do this in the first place?*

But I kept swimming and pushing the seaweed aside, hoping to see something of interest, and all at once I found myself in a bright clearing. And there, spiraling up from the depths and past me to the surface, was an enormous stingray, accompanied, up against her white underside, by a much smaller ray, her pup. Had I not left my friend and risked getting lost and groped my way through the slimy kelp, I would never have seen them.

I groped my way back to God first by asking believers questions and paging through the less mystifying parts of the Bible. Soon, I acquiesced to an invitation to attend a Bible study. I couldn't pray, really—not, at least, as I understood prayer at the time—but I woke in the night and worried about matters of my existence and, hesitantly at first, pondered what might be known about God. I thought back over my past and marveled over the many moments when I had been, as it seemed to me, magically protected from dangers and sorrows of my own creating. Somehow, I began to value the very life I was living, to see it new. It was like getting up after a long convalescence, feeling weak but blissfully conscious of the beginnings of wellness.

Slowly, hardly realizing what I was sensing, I became aware of a force for good behind it all. Not mere luck. And certainly not a reward for any good conduct on my part. More like an old aunt whom I had long since forgotten existed but who had never forgotten me. Despite my silence and neglect, she sent her yearly Christmas cards, inside of which I could depend on finding a folded up check. "Your aunt was telling me how wonderful you were," other relatives reported. And when the aunt died, though I had not seen her in a lifetime, she left me everything she had. I started to sense a presence in my life something like such an aunt, a benevolent being, far away but ever devoted and inexplicably interested in what was going on in my life.

The Bible, meanwhile, offered those promises. *I will not forsake you. I will send a comforter, an advocate. I will be with you always.* And one day my longing was transformed into a more specific hope that the promises were true. And hope, I learned in a passage I came upon in the Bible study I was attending—a passage I have since relied on again and again—was the armature of faith: "Now faith is being sure of what we hope for and certain of what we do not see" (Hebrews 11:1). Although I couldn't see or hear or touch God, I became increasingly convinced of that hand of protection. The hand that wrote those little checks, year after year. The voice that spoke well of me, despite my meanness and neglect. The hope that, independent of my own plans or attention, sought to change my future with an unmerited inheritance.

Hope is a complicated word in English. In one sense—the most common sense in which the word is used in contemporary English, I would argue—*hope* means a desire or wish for something that you don't have. In this sense, the word is an expression of longing and uncertainty. In earlier versions of English, *hope* meant the opposite: to have confidence or trust. The archaic sense, I'm guessing, is the sense modern Bible translators intend when they use *hope* in the definition of faith in Hebrews 11:1—Now faith is being sure of what we hope for—and also in Paul's identification of "faith, hope, and love" as key Christian traits in I Corinthians 13:13. The *hope* of the Bible, in other words, is not the hesitant longing we all have for the promises of scripture—that we may survive death and be eternally loved—but rather the certainty of their fulfillment. *To hope,* in the biblical sense, is not merely to long for God's presence but to grope for it. To reach out for or feel after it. To find God, in other words, we must step out of mere passive desire and into trust. We must do the work of believing by seeking evidence that the promises are true. We must, in the archaic sense, *hope* God into our company.

And God hopes, too, in every sense of the word. According to Paul, God choreographed all of human experience "so that" people "would seek him and perhaps reach out for him and find him, though he is not far from any one of us" (Acts 17:27). *Perhaps. Perhaps* we would grope about, in our blindness and self-obsession. *Perhaps* we would reach out for the God who hovers near us all, longing for *our* notice, *our* company, *our* presence. Paul's description of God evokes a good deal of uncertainty and longing on the part of the all-knowing, all-powerful one whose company we seek. The God whose presence we hope for also hopes for our company.

My own words here astonish me. It may be blasphemy—surely the force that brought the entire universe and us into existence cannot be reduced to a being so vulnerable as to hope, often in vain, for our attention—but that's the God I eventually came to believe in. The divine presence in which I now bask, when I let myself be certain that God's promises are true, is the presence of one who longs for *my* presence. To believe in God as an adult—and to continue to sense God's enduring presence in my daily life—amounts not merely to longing for God but to reaching out and embracing these amazing hopes and claiming them as real. God will never abandon me. The Holy Spirit is hourly employed in comforting and guiding me and intervening on my behalf. Jesus is with me, right now, just as he said he would be. However I fail to live up to God's high standards—and I will fail—I am not and will never be forsaken.

When I look back over the period of God's disappearance from my life, from that first sense of absence in my conversations with God to the involuntary longing that consumed me in the lonely years that followed, I see beneath the spiritual deadness the live skeleton of God's plan. I hear, in retrospect, God's voice heartening me, just as God encouraged the Israelites in their Babylonian exile:

> This is what the LORD says: "When seventy years are completed for Babylon, I will come to you and fulfill my good promise to bring you back to this place. For I know the plans I have for you," declares the LORD, "plans to prosper you and not to harm you, plans to give you hope and a future. Then you will call on me and come and pray to me, and I will listen to you. You will seek me and find me when you seek me with all your heart. I will be found by you," declares the LORD, "and will bring you back from captivity. I will gather you from all the nations and places where I have banished you," declares the LORD, "and will bring you back to the place from which I carried you into exile." (Jeremiah 29:10–14)

Faith is a strange thing, it seems to me. It fills us with certainty, yet inches forward by means of doubts, musings, and hesitations. It is of God, and yet it is the work expected of us. Somehow we must learn to be "certain of what we do not see"—which, as the writer of Hebrews comments, "the ancients were commended for" (11:1–2). Faith is hoping and being certain *without* seeing or hearing or touching God. Though we long for faith and though it hovers close to us, always offered, nevertheless we have to grope for it, as for an unlit lantern in some dark outbuilding in the night. And some turn away before they find it. But, once grasped and fumbled to a flame, it has the potential to lead us out of the darkness into the star-filled night.

1 ❧ Consider a circumstance in which you would use the word *hope*. You may hope a beloved friend or relative will come and visit you. If you have a garden, you may hope for a rain to soften the soil enough that you can get rid of the weeds. If you are ill, you may hope that you will recover. Voice your hope out loud: *I hope I will get to see the one I love.* Or, *I hope it will rain. I hope I will get better.* Pay attention to how saying this sentence out loud makes you feel. Now, in your mind, transform the word *hope* into an expression of trust and confidence and restate your hope out loud. You might say, *I am confident that I will get to see the one I love.* Or, *I'm sure it's going to rain* or *I know that I will get well.* Even better, you might eliminate the trust language altogether and state the thing you hope for as a reality that is about to occur. *My friend is coming! It's about to rain! I'm getting better.* Consider how the transformation of the word *hope* as we usually use it (meaning *to desire* or *wish*) into its archaic sense (meaning *to trust* or *have confidence*) not only results in a difference in attitude toward the thing hoped for but also a difference in how you would act. In the case of merely desiring or wishing, you might not act at all. Having confidence, on the other hand, obligates you to get ready—to prepare a guest room or make space in your schedule for a day in the garden or figure out what you need to do to catch up after your illness.

2 ❧ Moving out of merely hoping for God's presence into confidence that you will find it will result in action on your part. Transform hope into trust in your search for God's presence as in exercise 1 by imagining that God really is present. Hovering near you at all times. Listening to your words. Sending you messages. Willing you to grope around and feel your way nearer. Consider—no, plan out—how God's actual presence will change what you do on a minute-to-minute basis.

3 ❧ Some colleagues of mine meet with students who are about to graduate but who, after four years at our Christian university, feel not more but less secure in their faith. As is common at their age, many of them are struggling as believers. Some have rejected the faith of their childhood altogether. Someone commented to me recently that these students, in contrast to how I describe my years of atheism, weren't struggling to believe at all. Rather than seeking evidence of God's presence, they were devoting a good deal of time and energy to seeking evidence that God does *not* exist. If, having read this book in the hope of locating God in your life, you still feel no closer to God and no more aware of God's presence, consider whether you might actually be investing more energy in resisting the notion that God is there than in actually seeking evidence of God's presence.

4 ❧ Be alert to the hallmarks of such a goal. Those who are working to disprove God's existence or presence in their lives often have ready arguments centering on some pet doctrine or aspect of faith, such as others' hypocrisy, the question of whether those who've never heard the gospel could be damned to an eternity in hell, the unreliability or inapplicability of scripture, or some denominational issue that upset them long in the past. They have often done considerable research in that one area of belief and may invest heavily in either avoiding others who disagree with them or else seeking them out and arguing with them. If you are struggling as a believer in this way, it will be hard for you to realize that you are. But try. More important, try to redirect some of the energy you are using to disprove God's existence toward seeking evidence of God's presence. Go outside. Read scripture. Listen to the faith stories of those around you. Remember instances when you have sensed God in the past. Intentionally seek out God among the needy. Above all, pay attention to your life. May you be blessed with recognition of the abundant evidence of God's presence that surrounds you.

NOTES

Chapter One

[1] Joey Holder, "Unto the King" (Far Lane Music Publishing, 1984).

Chapter Two

[1] Jean Piaget, Chapter 1, "The Development of Object Concept," *The Construction of Reality in the Child* (*Construction du réel chez l'enfant*, 1937), translated by Margaret Cook (New York: Basic Books, 1954), 3–96.

[2] *Construction of Reality in the Child*, 60.

[3] *Voices Online Edition*, Vol. XX, No. 3, Christmas 2005/Epiphany 2006, www.wf-f.org/05-3-Communion.

Chapter Four

[1] Betty Edwards, Chapter 5, "Drawing on Memories: Your History As an Artist," *Drawing on the Right Side of the Brain* (New York: J. P. Tarcher, 1979).

[2] Daniel J. Simons and Christopher F. Chabris, *Gorillas in Our Midst: Sustained Inattentional Blindness for Dynamic Events* (*Perception*, Vol. 28, 1999), 1059–1074.

[3] Temple Grandin and Catherine Johnson, *Animals in Translation: Using the Mysteries of Autism to Decode Animals* (New York: Scribner, 2004), 51 [authors' italics].

[4] *Animals in Translation*, 51.

Chapter Six

[1] Martin Luther, *The Table Talk of Martin Luther* (*Tischreden*, compiled by Johannes Mathesius, 1566), translated by William Hazlitt (London: H. G. Bohn, 1857), 11.

Chapter Eight

[1] Augustine, Book X, "Memory," *The Confessions* (*Confessiones*, 398), Part I, *The Works of Saint Augustine: A Translation for the 21st Century*, translated by Maria Boulding, edited by John E. Rotelle (Hyde Park: New City Press, 1997).

[2] See Leo Tolstoy, *Confession* (1882); Hudson Taylor, *A Retrospect* (1894); Kathleen Norris, *Dakota: A Spiritual Geography* (1993); Anne Lamott, *Travelling Mercies: Some Thoughts on Faith* (1999); Nigel Slater, *Toast: The Story of a Boy's Hunger* (2004).

Chapter Nine

[1] Martin Luther, *A Treatise on Usury* (*[Grosser]Sermon von dem Wucher*, 1520), translated by Charles M. Jacobs, *Works of Martin Luther*, Volume IV (Philadelphia: A. J. Holman and the Castle Press, 1931), 37–38.

Chapter Ten

[1] Joseph P. Engles, *Catechism for Young Children: Being an Introduction to the Shorter Catechism* (Philadelphia: Presbyterian Board of Publication, 1840), 8.
[2] Marilynne Robinson, *Gilead* (New York: Farrar, Straus and Giroux, 2004), 124.

Chapter Eleven

[1] Wendell Berry, "Look Out," *Given: New Poems* (Washington, DC: Shoemaker & Hoard, 2005).

Chapter Twelve

[1] Brennan Manning, Staley Lecture, John Brown University, September 9, 2008; see also *The Ragamuffin Gospel* (1990).
[2] Robert K. Greenleaf, *Servant Leadership: A Journey into the Nature of Legitimate Power and Greatness* (New York: Paulist Press, 1977).

Chapter Fourteen

[1] All quotes, unless otherwise indicated, are from Mother Teresa and Brian Kolodiejchuk, *Come Be My Light: The Private Writings of the "Saint of Calcutta"* (New York: Doubleday, 2007).
[2] Saint John of the Cross, *Dark Night of the Soul* (*La noche oscura del alma*, circa 1576), translated by E. Allison Peers (New York: Image Books, 1959).
[3] Christopher Hitchens, *The Missionary Position: Mother Teresa in Theory and Practice* (London: Verso, 1997).
[4] Christopher Hitchens, "Teresa, Bright and Dark," *Newsweek Web Exclusive*. 29 August 2007, www.newsweek.com/id/38603.
[5] Christopher Hitchens, "Mommie Dearest," *Slate Magazine*, 20 October 2003, www.slate.com/id/2090083.
[6] Mother Teresa, *Love: A Fruit Always in Season: Daily Meditations from the Words of Mother Teresa of Calcutta*, edited and selected by Dorothy S. Hunt (San Francisco: Ignatius, 1987), 232.
[7] Mother Teresa, *No Greater Love*, edited by Becky Benenate and Joseph Durepos (Novato: New World Library, 1997), 13, 30.

[8] Mother Teresa, *The Nobel Peace Prize 1979: Nobel Lecture.* 11 December, 1979, http://nobelprize.org/nobel_prizes/peace/laureates/1979/teresa-lecture.
[9] *No Greater Love*, 28–29.
[10] Mother Teresa, *The Joy in Loving: A Guide to Daily Living with Mother Teresa*, compiled by Jaya Chaliha and Edward Le Joly (New York: Viking Penguin, 1997), 267.
[11] Mother Teresa, *A Simple Path*, compiled by Lucinda Vardey (New York: Ballantine, 1995), 74.
[12] *No Greater Love*, 34.
[13] *A Simple Path*, 36. [Some editions of this book include this quote, but, curiously, others do not.]
[14] *No Greater Love*, 13.

Chapter Fifteen

[1] Keith Green, "Create in Me a New Heart," *Jesus Commands Us To Go* (Last Days Ministries, 1984).
[2] John Gottman and Nan Silver, *Why Marriages Succeed or Fail: What You Can Learn from the Breakthrough Research to Make Your Marriage Last* (New York: Simon & Schuster, 1994), 93–98.